Municipal Management Series

Managing Local Government Finance: Cases in Decision Making

International City/County ICMA Management Association

The International City/County Management Association is the professional and educational organization for appointed administrators and assistant administrators in local government. The purposes of ICMA are to enhance the quality of local government and to nurture and assist professional local government administrators in the United States and other countries. To further its mission, ICMA develops and disseminates new approaches to management through training programs, information services, and publications.

Local government managers—carrying a wide range of titles—serve cities, towns, counties, councils of governments, and state/provincial associations of local governments. They serve at the direction of elected councils and governing boards. ICMA serves these managers and local governments through many programs that aim at improving the manager's professional competence and strengthening the quality of all local governments.

The International City/County Management Association was founded in 1914; adopted its City Management Code of Ethics in 1924; and established its Institute for Training in Municipal Administration in 1934. The institute, in turn, provided the basis for the Municipal Management Series, generally termed the "ICMA Green Books."

ICMA's interests and activities include public management education; standards of ethics for members; the *Municipal Year Book* and other data services; urban research; and newsletters, a monthly magazine, *Public Management*, and other publications. ICMA's efforts toward the improvement of local government management—as represented by this book—are offered for all local governments and educational institutions.

Editorial advisory board

Municipal Management Series

Managing Local Government Finance: Cases in Decision Making

**Published by the
International
City/County
Management
Association**

Editor

**James M. Banovetz
Northern Illinois University**

Municipal Management Series

Managing Local Government Finance: Cases in
  Decision Making

Advanced Supervisory Practices

Effective Communication: A Local Government Guide

The Effective Local Government Manager

Effective Supervisory Practices: Better Results through
  Teamwork

Emergency Management: Principles and Practice for Local
  Government

Local Government Police Management

Management of Local Planning

Management of Local Public Works

Management Policies in Local Government Finance

Managing Fire Services

Managing Local Government: Cases in Decision Making

Managing Small Cities and Counties: A Practical Guide

The Practice of Local Government Planning

The Practice of State and Regional Planning

Service Contracting: A Local Government Guide

Library of Congress Cataloging-in-Publication Data
Managing local government finance : cases in decision making / editor,
  James M. Banovetz.
      p.   cm. — (Municipal management series)
    ISBN 0-87326-111-9 (pbk.)
    1. Local finance — Decision making — Case studies.   2. Local
  government — Decision making — Case studies.   I. Banovetz, James M.
  II. International City/County Management Association.   III. Series.
  HJ9105.M324   1996
  352.1 — dc20   96-5647
                                                             CIP

Printed in the United States of America

99989796
54321

Foreword

This book is designed to give its readers a taste of the distinctive world of local government finance administration. The cases that make it up have been written to provide both the practicing local government administrator or finance officer, and the future local government administrator or finance officer, an opportunity and a context to visit some of the enduring problems of local government financial management, and to examine their own thinking about appropriate responses to such problems.

The book also is designed as a supplement for the standard course on budgeting and finance administration in the Master of Public Administration curriculum. As such, it is intended to help the typical M.P.A. curriculum better meet the *Guidelines for Local Government Management Education* adopted in 1992 by both the National Association of Schools of Public Affairs and Administration and the International City/County Management Association. Those guidelines, distributed by NASPAA along with its accreditation standards, suggest that, to prepare students for local government management careers, courses in the NASPAA core curriculum "should integrate local government concepts, issues, and examples so that local government management students are familiar with what is generic as well as distinct about the context and administration of local government."

As the guidelines note, "The local government environment is unique." Frederick C. Mosher, in his classic *Democracy and the Public Service*, made much the same point when he argued that city managers "remain almost the only generalist public administrative class in the nation." Such distinctiveness, the guidelines argue, must be imparted to those preparing to spend their careers in the administration of local government.

To achieve these purposes, and to bridge the gap between public finance administration in its generic and local government manifestations, this book presents six case studies that challenge the reader to apply financial management concepts within the policymaking environment of city and county government. At the same time, it introduces the reader to the complexity of political/administrative tasks—such as tax policy formation, revenue forecasting, and debt management—that are rarely encountered by administrators in most federal or state agencies, but which are routine challenges in local government.

These case studies capture the flavor of local management, not by giving readers information to use in solving problems, but rather by describing the complex legal, environmental, and human considerations that lead up to a managerial decision and then throwing the decision into the reader's lap. The cases thus provide a basis for simulated policy deliberation, not a formula for problem resolution. Each case concludes with a series of questions designed to foster and enrich the deliberative process.

To make the cases more challenging for student users, the decision actually made, and the resulting consequences, have not been included in this book.

The outcomes, or ''aftermaths'' have instead been compiled and are included in a supplement to this book, *Managing Local Government Finance: A Supplement*, which is available separately.

Each case presented in this book represents an actual, real-world situation that a local government manager had to resolve on the job. Most of the cases were written by or with the collaboration of the administrator involved, so problems and issues are presented as they were actually perceived by the person who had to decide and act.

ICMA is grateful to Dr. James M. Banovetz, who edited the book, and to a special editorial advisory board of university professors and local government administrators who selected the cases and whose insight and comments have been instrumental in developing the quality of this book.

Much of the early planning and design for the book was accomplished while the editor was serving in the Albert A. Levin Chair of Urban Studies and Public Service at the Maxine Goodman Levin College of Urban Affairs at Cleveland State University. Members of the editorial advisory board (with their affiliations at the time the work was performed) are Eric Anderson, City Manager, Evanston, Illinois; Larry Brown, County Administrator, Washtenaw County, Michigan; Claire Felbinger, Associate Professor and Director of the M.P.A. Program at Cleveland State University; Marilyn Leuck, City Manager, Hercules, California; James Svara, Professor of Public Administration and Director of the M.P.A. Program at North Carolina State University; and Charles Washington, Professor of Public Administration at Florida Atlantic University.

Editorial direction and supervision for the preparation of this book was provided by Barbara H. Moore, Director of ICMA's Municipal Management Series, of which this book is a part. June Kubasiak of Northern Illinois University managed the communications and provided support services to the manuscript development and referee process. Other staff who worked directly on the production of the book included Dawn M. Leland, Eileen Hughes, and Julie L. Butler of ICMA.

William H. Hansell, Jr.
Executive Director

International City/County
Management Association

Contents

Matrix of coverage

A major advantage of the case approach to teaching is the flexibility it offers the instructor. A good case can often be used to provide instruction on different topics, or on a number of topics simultaneously. The following matrix lists topics that are typically covered in a course on budgeting and finance, with an indication of how each of these cases might be used. This matrix also shows some of the other basic topics in public management that are addressed by each case.

Subject	Case number					
1. Kind and level of government						
County	1				5	
Small city			3	4		
Medium city		2				6
Large city	1					
2. The context of government						
Politics	1	2			5	
Administration and politics		2			5	
Intergovernmental relations	1	2				
Public policymaking	1	2		4		6
Government and the economy		2	3			
3. Budgeting and finance						
Tax policy	1	2	3	4		
Public revenues	1	2	3	4		6
Economic forecasting		2	3			
Assessing financial condition	1	2	3	4		6
Revenue forecasting	1	2	3			
Economic development	1	2	3			
Budgeting				4		6
Cost/benefit analysis		2	3		5	
Budget formulation				4		6
Budget administration					5	
Program analysis/evaluation			3		5	
Capital budgeting				4		6
Budget implementation					5	
Debt management						6
Capital financing				4		6
4. General management						
Organization theory			3		5	
Bureaucracy					5	
Managerial policymaking		2	3	4	5	
Use of consultants			3		5	

Introduction

The problem of money

A fundamental problem facing virtually every individual and every organization is money: where to get it, how to get more, where to keep it, how to protect it, what records to maintain, how to divide it among desired uses, where to spend it, how to get maximum benefit from it, and how to account for what happened to it. None of these are easy questions, even for a single individual living on a substantial income.

For local governments, which handle millions of dollars a year to provide benefits to thousands of people, such questions are staggering: they arise constantly, they can never be fully answered to everyone's satisfaction, and most of them are questions about which reasonable people may reasonably differ.

But such questions must be answered, regularly and routinely, in the daily operations of local governments. Sometimes the answers can be found in well-established procedures. Answers to many accounting questions, for instance, can be found in the work products of such organizations as the Governmental Accounting Standards Board, the Government Finance Officers Association, and the American Institute of Certified Public Accountants. But the solutions to many other financial management problems are not so accessible: questions of operating strategies, policy options, interpretation of standards, appropriate methodologies, and interpersonal relations pose issues that challenge the art as well as the science of financial management.

Such issues provide the "stuff" with which this book deals, and it deals with this "stuff" specifically within the context of contemporary local government.

The problem of local government

Within the sphere of public sector activity, local government poses a unique context for financial management. Unlike state and federal governments, in which elected officials interact in a capital city removed from the immediate environs of the people being represented and served, local governments operate "where the people are." As urbanologist David Churchill once remarked, "The city is the people." His statement applies equally well to counties.

The proximity of the people makes a huge difference. To the people, state and federal policymakers are names and television images who make policy and manage tax dollars in distant capitals and work with sums of money so huge as to be beyond the comprehension of the average person. Local government officials, however, are people who live and work in the neighborhood; they are on the streets and in the stores, clubs, and churches of the community; frequently they know and are known by a large percentage of the people whose money they are managing. They truly exercise the "sacred trust" described by Woodrow Wilson in his famous 1887 essay launching professional public administration in the United States.

Such proximity to the people has an impact on government managers. The influence of the people is felt much more routinely—and much more directly. The voice of the people is not something experienced only through newspaper articles, letters from constituents, conversations with lobbyists, and contacts back home during breaks in legislative sessions. For the local official, the voice of the people is also expressed by the citizens who attend council and committee meetings, the reports of citizens' advisory boards and commissions, the constituents who drop by the office or call on the telephone, and the conversations taking place at meetings of local clubs and civic organizations in which the official is participating. Local officials feel political pressure, not just through such appropriate channels, but also through constituent interruptions as they go about their daily routine, through unkind comments made to their spouses and children, and even through harassing phone calls in the wee hours of the night.

Professional staff, too, feel more direct pressure in local government than they do in federal or state service. They frequently live in the community and encounter the same pressures in their private lives. Further, because they are typically unprotected by civil service, and because their role in dealing with contentious local issues is so exposed to the public, the senior management staff of city and county governments find their jobs are at political risk to a degree unparalleled by their counterparts in federal, state, or even other kinds of local governments (such as school districts). City managers, as a group, experience a level of involuntary job turnover far in excess of that encountered by any other group of professional public administrators in the United States.

And much of the stress and job insecurity facing the local government manager/finance officer stems from issues involving money.

The problem of money and local government

Not only are money problems perva-

sive and political processes unique at the local government level, but the task of managing local government finance is distinctive. It is unusual in its range of responsibility: tax policy, revenue estimation and collection, treasury management, financial planning, capital budgeting, debt policy, debt management, expenditure allocation policy, budget policy, expenditure analysis and control, accountability, and auditing. While all governments perform all of these functions, only city and county governments concentrate so much of this responsibility in the hands of so few people. The local government manager/finance officer is verily a "jack of all financial trades."

Local government financial management is also distinctive in the interpersonal intensity of its politics. Local government administrators work in close proximity to each other. Tensions between them represent more than just job-related stress; at the local level, such tensions threaten to spill over into administrators' social and personal lives as well. To make matters worse, when the tensions are between elected and administrative officials, they pose a potentially severe threat to the job security of the latter.

Finally, local government financial management is distinctive because it contains a comparatively high risk component. There is an old saying among city managers that allegations of money mismanagement will get one in more trouble more quickly than any other kind of management shortcoming. Poor street construction or park management is harder to define, harder to quantify and measure, more difficult to document. Mismanagement where money is concerned is easier to define, easier to quantify and measure, easier to document—and provokes a much quicker report of scandal in the local press. From an elected official's perspective, financial mismanagement on the part of an appointed manager is very difficult to explain, impossible to defend, and certain grounds for a swift and unpleasant reaction.

All of these considerations, taken together, make the job of financial management in local government both more demanding and more challenging than in state or federal service.

By looking at financial management problems in local government, this book attempts to capture some of these nuances. Cases 1, 2, 3, and 6 describe elements of uniqueness in local government finance. Cases 4 and 5, the budgeting cases, deal with problems common to administrators at all levels of government, but they also demonstrate the complexity of the challenge of financial management at the community level. All of these cases give the reader a ''flavor'' of local financial management.

These cases provide insights into other dimensions of local government man-agement as well. They highlight the common gap between rational or good government behavior and politically acceptable behavior in the local government world; describe some of the complexities of relations between units of local government; provide insights into the use of external consultants; show how the art and science of public administration are different and where each is most applicable; and demonstrate the linkage between finance and planning.

Most of all, these cases clearly depict local government as both an arena of vast and complex professional challenges and a vehicle for improving the quality of life in the nation's neighborhoods.

James M. Banovetz

1 Formulating revenue policy

Editor's introduction

The one constant in American local government as the Twentieth Century winds down is financial pressure. Always in short supply, local government revenues are under increasing pressure to sustain public services in the wake of cutbacks in federal and state spending. Making matters still worse for local governments are two other realities:

1. The same voter resistance to taxes that is forcing cutbacks in state and federal spending also exists at the local level, making it equally difficult for city and county governments to increase their tax levies.
2. Local governments are the governments of last resort. Federal and state governments can reduce their spending for such public services as welfare, education, public safety, and infrastructure improvements. By default, this passes more responsibility for such services to governments at lower levels. But city and county governments are the lowest levels; they are charged by law with responsibility for the public welfare and safety. Theirs is the responsibility of first response to the problems of everyday life caused by hunger, illiteracy, crime, and unsafe public facilities. They are the last resort for dealing with basic societal problems.

City and county governments cannot pass the buck; they must satisfy at least the minimal service needs of their residents. Despite their resistance to taxes, the voters demand that local government respond to such needs. Further, the courts as well as public opinion hold local governments liable for failure to protect the public's well-being. Neither the courts nor the public have demonstrated any inclination to accept popular resistance to higher taxes as a legitimate excuse for government failure to respond adequately to human crises.

The reality of this situation creates a real quandary for local government leadership. This quandary is marvelously portrayed in the first case in this book, "County Options: To Tax or Not to Tax." Faced with declining intergovernmental revenues and state-imposed limitations on existing tax levies, the governments of Fleming County have experienced ten years of erosion in the purchasing power of their annual revenues, ten years of service cuts and postponed infrastructure maintenance, and a future that promises more of the same. State law permits Fleming County governments to levy a local income tax, but local political pressures have kept that from happening.

This is the story of one city whose governmental and civic leaders have "bitten the bullet" and advocated an income tax, but who can't unilaterally levy the tax without the cooperation of at least one other large local government in the county. Thus, the problem requires more than local statesmanship and courage; it requires intergovernmental cooperation as well. Adding a good dose of partisan political differences to the problem compounds the difficulties.

At first reading, it would appear that this is a poor case because the best option facing the decision makers seems so self-evident. But this is the reaction of the classroom, not of the real world. The fact that the best options appear obvious does not increase their political viability, especially in a time of taxpayer hostility toward government and resistance to new taxes. The obvious option in this situation, for instance, is made nearly impossible by past political failure and the bitter knowledge that successive failures only render any eventual passage of a tax even more unlikely.

What makes this case valuable is that the core problem it poses is widespread among local governments today, and the options for the problem's resolution nearly everywhere are just as risky and impossible as the alternatives outlined here.

This case, in short, encapsulates the challenge of governing in a time in which the ''professional'' or ''good government'' solution is neither politically viable nor popularly acceptable.

Welcome to the world of local government finance.

Case 1
County options: To tax or not to tax
Leda McIntyre Hall

Background

Guy Myers is in his second term as mayor of Saylor Park, a mid-sized midwestern town. Having served as the city's comptroller prior to his election, Myers has brought a clear understanding of the city's finances to his office. Here, as in other cities, the amount of federal dollars available to municipalities has shrunk drastically, and state support is now level at best. The state property tax freeze, which was passed almost twenty years ago, further complicates the financial situation in Saylor Park. During Myers's first term, city revenue was level, but the past two years have seen a serious decline in the real purchasing power of the city's budget. Programs have been cut, vacant positions usually are left unfilled, fewer new police officers are hired than are needed, and most capital projects have been put on hold.

Mayor Myers chairs Saylor Park's city council, which has nine elected council-members. He directs the city's administrative operations with the assistance of Scott Anderson, the senior professional administrator in the city's employment.

Saylor Park is one of two fairly large cities in Fleming County (population 247,000). There are 110,000 residents in Saylor Park, 40,000 residents in Landis, and the remaining residents live either in rural areas or in one of the six other incorporated places in the county. Having three major but separate administrative units (Saylor Park, Landis, and the county government) in the county complicates cooperation and fosters duplication.

Completely surrounded by Saylor Park, Landis is fairly parochial and has many residents of Belgian and Italian descent. The minority population is very small. On the socioeconomic scale, Landis tips toward the middle or upper-middle class and sees itself as a working-class, conservative town. Although little overt hostility exists between Landis and Saylor Park, Landis seeks to remain politically and socially independent from its larger neighbor. It operates under a mayor-council form of government, including a nine-member city council, without the assistance of a professional administrator.

Of the three formal governmental units, Fleming County is the oldest and traces its authority to the state constitution. Seven county commissioners share administrative and legislative authority over land use, the county jail, parks, and the sheriff's office. There is no county administrator or elected executive, a situation that creates a leadership void in the county. Property taxes are relatively low in the county, and its residents sometimes are accused of enjoying the benefits of Saylor Park and Landis without paying a share of the costs.

Local elections in the state are partisan. Guy Myers is a Democrat, Anne Wunker of Landis is a moderate Republican, and the Fleming County commissioners are conservative Republicans. As one might imagine, fierce partisan squabbling erupts whenever county-wide budgetary decisions must be made.

A proposed local-option income tax

At the time of the case, Myers and the Saylor Park City Council are preparing to approve a local-option income tax. State law allows local governments to impose one or more of a variety of local-option taxes, including an auto excise tax, a general income tax, an income tax earmarked for economic development, and an income tax that both provides general revenue and reduces property taxes. The preference of Mayor Myers and the city council is to adopt a combination of general and economic development taxes to compensate for shrinking general revenues and to finance repairs on local infrastructure, which has aged in some cases to an almost dangerous extent.

State law requires that two of the legislative bodies representing at least 51 percent of the population affected by a proposed tax adopt the local-option tax ordinance. In the case of Fleming County and its two fairly sizable cities, two of three legislative bodies involved would have to adopt the same local income tax ordinance. There is clear agreement among legislators in Saylor Park and general agreement in Landis that more revenue is needed, but the county commissioners are not so convinced. And there is little apparent consensus on the type of tax— if any—to be imposed.

Following the defeat last year of a similar local income tax proposal, each of the major jurisdictions announced cuts in expenditures. Saylor Park reduced the number of new police officers hired from fourteen to seven, cancelled nine neighborhood summer recreation programs, left four firefighter positions unfilled, and did not fill ten vacancies created by retirements in various agencies. Discussion also began on eliminating the city's solid waste division and contracting out for that service. Summer hours for city swimming pools were reduced by 30 percent. Fees at city golf courses rose by 20 percent, and discussion commenced about privatizing the golf courses.

The city of Landis started a mandatory recycling program and a monthly fee of $8 for trash pickup. A charge based on mileage was announced for the fire department's EMS transportation to area hospitals. A citywide hiring freeze was implemented, and other cuts still are being debated.

Fleming County announced that it would reduce the number of county park employees by 50 percent and cut back the hours that parks are open. Bonds have been approved for the construction of a new jail and juvenile facility, but insufficient funds exist to operate either facility. The shortage is projected to total more than $3.5 million within the next five years. Vacancies in county agencies created by retirements or resignations are not being filled. And the individual fare for public bus transportation has been raised from sixty cents to seventy-five cents.

A task force studying the situation found that efficiency measures have not been enough. Cutback strategies have led to atrophy of services and infrastructure. The task force observed several damaging trends: governments in the county are not offering employees cost-of-living increases in wages, bills are not being paid on time, reserves are becoming depleted, needed repairs and renovation projects are getting delayed, and little investment is being made in capital improvements.

The financial situation in Fleming County

Property taxes are the primary source of revenue for local governments in the state. These taxes, however, are subject to a freeze that was adopted nineteen years ago by the state legislature and that limits the annual increase in the tax levy. The purchasing power of the property tax levy can be calculated in one of two ways: (1) by dividing the actual levy by population (per capita), or (2) by using an index of real prices. Following the tax freeze, the purchasing power of the property tax levy in Fleming County fell dramatically for six years, then increased in the following ten years. Three years ago, the property tax levy purchased a bit more in government services than it did sixteen years earlier. Figure 1 illustrates the fluctuation in purchasing power of the property tax levy over this sixteen-year period.

Although county population grew little during this time, double-digit inflation plagued the county during most of the decade after the freeze was adopted. The property tax levy did not keep pace with inflation for two reasons. First, reassessments of real property are conducted infrequently—only in the first year of each decade. Reassessments update the assessed value for replacement costs and represent the only opportunity to adjust the real property tax base for inflation. Second, because reassessments primarily reflect new construction and changes in land classifications, inflation in real property values almost never allows growth in the maximum levy.

According to state law, the county levy may rise annually by the three-year average increase in assessed value, excluding reassessment years. The minimum rise is 5 percent, and the maximum is 10 percent. For almost all local governments in the state, the three-year average rise in assessed value is less than 5 percent, so the 5 percent minimum acts as a cap on the levy. Fleming County's allowable annual levy increase has not exceeded 5 percent since the property tax freeze was adopted. Obviously, political jurisdictions in the county need new sources of revenue just to hold the line.

Local income tax options

Legislation allowing a *county adjusted gross income tax (CAGIT)* was passed twenty years ago. Although the bulk of CAGIT revenue must be used to reduce property taxes, local governments are allowed to use some of it in their general budgets. The possible rates for county residents are 0.50, 0.75, or 1.00 percent.

Figure 1 Fleming County's real per-capita property tax levy

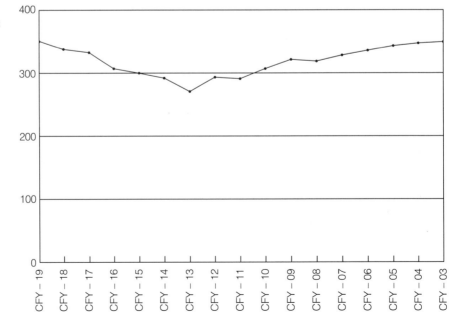

Note: "CFY" refers to current fiscal year. Thus, "CFY-19" refers to current fiscal year minus 19 years.

CAGIT can be adopted by the county commissioners without the consent of either city council.

The state legislature authorized a *county option income tax (COIT)* ten years ago. Technically, it is imposed by a COIT Council, which has 100 votes divided among local fiscal officials based on their jurisdictions' shares of the county's population. This division of votes by population is the legal provision that effectively requires two of the three legislative bodies in Fleming County to approve a tax because none of the three represents more than 51 percent of the county's population. A 0.2 percent tax is allowed in the first year, with 0.1 percent annual increases allowed, to a maximum of 1 percent. COIT revenue is spendable and is not tied to property tax relief.

Six years ago, the legislature authorized local adoption of an *economic development income tax (EDIT)*. If the county commission approves a county adjusted gross income tax (CAGIT), the commission later can impose an EDIT. If there is a COIT Council in place, it must approve the EDIT. Any legislative body in the county may approve an EDIT for its jurisdiction if no other income taxes have been assessed. Receipts from an EDIT, with a maximum rate of 0.5 percent, must be used for economic development or capital projects. No automatic property tax relief is included.

Counties can adopt any local-option income tax or a combination of CAGIT and EDIT *or* COIT and EDIT. Because the state allows local-option income taxes, almost all of the state's seventy-seven counties have adopted one or more local options (see Figure 2).

Fleming County is one of the nine counties in the state with no local income taxes. A study completed three years ago reported that taxable income in Fleming County the year before was $2,488.6 million and that it had been increasing at a rate of about 7 percent each year. The state department of commerce estimated that if this rate of increase continued, taxable income three years ago would have been $3,048.6 million. Thus, conservative estimates suggest that a 1.00 percent local income tax would generate $30.5 million; a 1.25 percent combination of CAGIT and EDIT would raise $38.1 million; or a 0.50 percent tax would generate $15.2 million. Each income tax has a formula by which funds are shared among the fiscal jurisdictions, but each would provide jurisdictions either with property tax relief and general revenue, or with economic development funds and general revenue.

Local income tax KO'd

Two years ago, Mayor Myers succeeded in having a combination COIT and EDIT proposal introduced and ratified by a 9-to-0 vote of the Saylor Park City Council. The proposal lost 6-to-3 when voted on by the Landis City Council, and the Fleming County Commission never brought the issue to a vote.

A COIT Council was established, with votes divided as illustrated in Figure 3, based on the share of the county's population represented by a fiscal body. In most counties in the state, a single fiscal body has a majority of the votes, but Fleming County is one of a few counties in which no one body has a majority, so a coalition is needed to pass a COIT. The county commission and the city councils of Saylor

Figure 2 Local income tax adoptions in the state, as of the current year		
	CAGIT only	36
	CAGIT and EDIT	9
	COIT only	17
	COIT and EDIT	3
	EDIT only	3
	Total localities with income taxes	68
	Total localities without income taxes	9

Figure 3   Division of votes
on the COIT Council

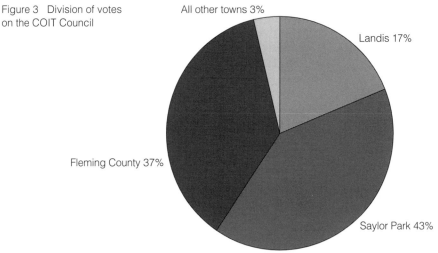

All other towns 3%

Landis 17%

Fleming County 37%

Saylor Park 43%

Park and Landis have 96.6 percent of the votes, and any two of those three bodies together could enact the COIT.

Last year, Saylor Park once again passed a COIT and EDIT combination. The income taxes were endorsed by the chamber of commerce, the seven school districts in the county, local unions, and the *Saylor Park Sentry*. Some opposition arose from a citizen group, but no significant remonstrance was mounted at the city council meeting. As with the previous proposal, the council voted 9-to-0 to approve the tax.

The county commission brought the proposal to a vote a few days before the Landis City Council meeting. Remarkably, one commissioner offered an amendment to the proposal suggesting that the commission go on record not only as opposing the income tax but also as refusing to accept the county's share of income tax revenues, should both major city councils pass the proposal. After some discussion, this amendment was defeated, and the income tax proposal met a similar fate, 7-to-0.

It appeared that Mayor Anne Wunker had the votes on the Landis City Council to ratify the proposal and, in conjunction with the Saylor Park vote, to adopt a local income tax in Fleming County. Mayor Myers telephoned Mayor Wunker several times in the days leading up to the vote: "Look, Anne, we're out on a limb on this issue once again. It's clear to me that Saylor Park residents are solidly behind this. We both have a general idea of what will happen at the county commission, so it's up to you. Do you think the votes are there to support the taxes?"

Anne Wunker grimaced. She knew that Foster Willson, a newly elected Democrat on the city council, would be the swing vote. He had publicly promised the mayor his support for the income tax proposal, but he might waver. "Guy, I have firm support from four councilmembers and fairly certain opposition from four others," Mayor Wunker replied. "Last week, after your vote, Willson stopped by to say I could count on him. A couple of days ago, he said he was still deciding. This morning, I had him in for coffee, and he said he'd go along with the tax proposal even though he had some misgivings." Heavy lobbying and a huge, hostile audience on the night of the vote, however, apparently swayed Willson because his negative vote led to a 5-to-4 defeat for the COIT/EDIT package in Landis.

What is clear from this series of votes is that a majority of legislators—and both mayors—favored the COIT/EDIT package. Tallying all the votes, the tax package would have passed 14-to-11. The political frustration is obvious. For those who support a local income tax, the maxim "United we stand, divided we fall" rings true.

The case: Who will lead the charge?

Currently, governmental jurisdictions in Fleming County face combined revenue shortfalls for the fiscal year of nearly $40 million. Intergovernmental revenue as a share of local government budgets continues to decline, and this decrease is exacerbated by state mandates, primarily involving entitlement programs. Capital projects that have been neglected for the past five years face extended waiting periods. A report from a local research institute laments that ''. . . we are disinvesting in our communities.''

Fleming County's political jurisdictions are faced with crumbling bridges, roads in desperate need of repair, declining economic development, parks with reduced hours, and cuts in basic services. These trends will make it more difficult to attract businesses and new residents. It is a precarious time.

One study suggests five alternatives:

1. Continue to cut services.
2. Rely on property taxes.
3. Hope that the federal and state governments will change their policies and increase intergovernmental aid.
4. Search for ways to make government more efficient.
5. Adopt some version of a local income tax.

The Fleming County Chamber of Commerce has established a task force on local funding and charged it with analyzing and reviewing revenue options, needs, uses, and sources for the county. The task force is to make recommendations to the chamber's board of directors for action. An early report from the task force suggests that the study of possible funding sources may result in several recommendations:

1. Make no change in current fiscal and finance policy.
2. Determine/identify possible fiscal inefficiencies.
3. Expand current funding sources or alternatives.
4. Identify/evaluate funding sources from outside the immediate community.
5. Identify/evaluate new local funding sources.

In a speech to the state legislature, the chairperson of the state senate's finance committee made a clear response to requests for increased aid by local governments. Those counties having a local income tax—generously allowed by the legislature—would achieve favored county status when future allocations were made. Counties unwilling to adopt local measures to meet local needs would be told to go to the end of the budgetary line. It is likely that the chairperson looked directly at officials from the nine recalcitrant counties as he made this point. They could not have misunderstood.

One might conclude that the handwriting is on the wall: the most effective approach is the adoption of a local income tax. It remains to be seen whether or not the necessary votes can be obtained in the city councils and county commission.

Intergovernmental ideas

Administrators in Fleming County have made some attempts to streamline services and make government more efficient. Five years ago, the county and Saylor Park agreed to merge their building departments, consolidating zoning, permits, and other regulatory functions under a single administrative umbrella. Regulatory consistency improved, and substantial savings were realized both in the county and in Saylor Park.

Under new fire safety regulations passed by the state three years ago, all towns and cities with a population of 40,000 or greater were required to add an extension ladder truck. This kind of truck enables rescue operations in buildings more than three stories tall—a safety consideration apparently assumed by the state to become important as towns grow. Three years ago, neither fire department affected, Saylor Park or Landis, owned a truck that met the new requirement. In a cost-saving move, the two cities agreed to purchase one truck and divide the $480,000 price on a per-capita basis. To facilitate sharing, the truck is housed in a Saylor Park fire station near the Landis city limits.

Recently, representatives from the purchasing departments of Landis, Saylor Park, and Fleming County began formal discussions on consolidating their functions into a single county-wide agency. While huge cost savings are unlikely, such an agreement would improve the buying power of all jurisdictions involved and would streamline purchasing details.

There have been informal discussions about consolidating the park systems of the county, Landis, and Saylor Park. As of the current fiscal year, each system has its own administration, program, and maintenance staff, and each has a user fee scale in place that charges more to residents of other jurisdictions. Parks in all three places are used heavily. After the defeat of last year's local income tax proposal, park budgets universally were targeted for cuts. Persuasive arguments can be made that the park systems should merge. Residents of Landis, however, are expected to oppose such a merger, so that designing a truly county-wide proposal would be a difficult task.

Deadlines and interest groups

It is November. State law requires that an affirmative vote of the COIT Council be recorded by March 31 of the next year in order to enact a local income tax with collections beginning June 1.

Because of the division of votes on the COIT Council, someone needs to facilitate and sponsor the introduction of a local income tax. In the past, Mayor Guy Myers has stepped forward to assume that role. Because Saylor Park has the largest population of the three primary jurisdictions as well as the most to lose in city services, capital projects, and economic development issues, the pressure is on Myers to manage the fight. Leadership responsibilities could be divided among Myers, Wunker, other political leaders in the county, and the chamber. Certainly, a coalition would be a positive force. But two facts continue to be problematic. First, there is no single leader to marshal support or to speak for the county government. Second, administrative staff and the chamber are not being used to their full potential because Myers does not want to give the impression that he plans to bully the tax through the legislative process.

Last week, the three major unions in Saylor Park—the Fraternal Order of Police, the International Association of Firefighters, and the Teamsters—sent a unified group of representatives to urge the mayor to reintroduce a combined COIT and EDIT. They pledged to support councilmembers who voted for the taxes and promised to continue meeting with their counterparts in Landis.

Just this morning, the editor of the *Saylor Park Sentry* called to tell Myers that the Sunday editorial would urge county political officials to "do the right thing" by approving a county income tax package. In reply, Myers made no comment other than to agree with the editor's position.

Mayor Myers has returned from lunch with the president of the chamber of commerce. Although the chamber's support is assured and would become public at the mayor's request, Myers has asked the group to refrain from public statements or endorsements of a local income tax for a few weeks.

The decision problem

Guy Myers really has not asked to be the leader of the fight for a local income tax. True, he campaigned the first time on a platform that included expanding the city's vision for financing public services. Clearly, he initiated the local income tax ordinance that had been defeated. And the Saylor Park City Council, Myers's staff, many elected city officials, and a majority of the mayor's constituents have endorsed the income tax proposal.

The bottom line is that Saylor Park has to have one or more new sources of revenue. A local income tax would benefit Saylor Park as well as the rest of the county. Defending the proposal is not a clear political risk for Myers, but it might be for some of the city councilmembers and for Wunker, and it certainly is for the county commissioners.

Choosing a course of action will not be easy. Mayor Myers has several options:

1. Long committed to seeking innovative solutions, Myers could lead the way once again by persuading the Saylor Park City Council to pass a local income tax proposal and cast a 43 percent "yes" vote with the COIT Council.
2. Because the chamber of commerce board has offered assistance, Myers could ask its members to intervene with reluctant councilmembers on the Landis City Council. Perhaps chamber members could wield more influence over individual councilmembers than Myers could.
3. Myers also could give the chamber a green light to lobby and advertise in support of the income tax proposal. The chamber has offered to fund an advertising campaign advocating the EDIT portion of the proposal and, implicitly, the COIT as well.

   The proposed strategy is modeled on another county's plan. One of the most recent counties to assess a local income tax had marketed the package assertively. There, the chamber had written a slogan, created an eye-catching logo, and spent several thousand dollars in newspaper and radio advertising. Chamber members made a "needs list" with two or three items from each political jurisdiction in the county and successfully sold the local income tax to county residents as a way to meet those *specific* needs. Even though there was no public referendum, voters were aware of the need for a new tax and communicated their support to the council. Maybe the idea would work in Fleming County.
4. Myers could attack the county commissioners for stonewalling previous proposals and could demand publicly that the commissioners show their plans for funding county services.

Mayor Myers sought the counsel of his senior administrative adviser, Scott Anderson. "Scott," he asked, "would you give my dilemma some thought? We both know that Saylor Park needs a major new source of revenue; we know that new state aid is likely to be minimal unless the county or Landis joins with us in levying some form of income tax. You know the history of our efforts here. You know that the Republicans on the county commission will be a very hard sell on any tax increase, especially in these antitax times. You know that the chamber will move heaven and earth to help us pass a new tax package and that the newspaper will support it. But you also know that too much public effort by the chamber could backfire with the voters.

"Our problem here is both political and intergovernmental. We have the necessary political support in Saylor Park, but we can't move without support from Landis or Fleming County and preferably from both.

"Complicating our problem is the probability that the next effort to get an optional tax will be our last. If we are defeated twice, there will be no hope for a third attempt, at least not while you and I are around. Yet, we can't provide good public services without more money; we can't do the jobs we want to do unless we get an income tax. We really can't delay the task of finding more revenue.

"I need your advice on three questions. First, strategically, should we proceed even if Landis supports us but the county commission does not? Second, how much of a leadership role should I play in this next county-wide effort? Finally, how do you think a public campaign should be organized and orchestrated to achieve our objective?

"Please take some time to think about this, and let's meet next week to discuss your ideas."

Suddenly, the mayor's problem was Anderson's problem. Anderson had just heard, at a municipal conference, that one way in which professional administrators can succeed is to help their elected bosses feel successful in their governing efforts. The mayor had just asked him to help solve this dilemma. How should he proceed, and what, if anything, should he advise?

Discussion questions

1. Should a professional administrator advise an elected official on a matter of political strategy such as this? Why or why not? If so, are there any limitations on the kinds of advice that can be given? For instance, can Anderson advise the mayor on the political consequences for him personally if he assumes leadership of the income tax campaign? If not, how should Anderson explain his position to the mayor?

2. What kind of role, if any, is appropriate for Anderson to play personally in the design and implementation of a campaign to secure approval for an income tax package?

The next questions can be answered from either the perspective of Mayor Myers or that of Administrator Anderson, depending upon the reader's response to the first two questions.

3. Should the mayor recommend a local income tax package to the Saylor Park City Council? Which taxes should the proposal contain?

4. Public services will suffer and decline if new revenue sources are not identified. The county's infrastructure and criminal justice systems are dangerously underfunded. Are there ethical considerations involved? How far should tax advocates go to achieve passage of new taxes?

5. Evaluate each option that the mayor is considering. What are the strengths and weaknesses of each?

6. How could Mayor Myers engage the chamber, legislative supporters, and local activists in a public education process? What services could be offered in a package to the public that would elicit enough voter support to influence reluctant legislators?

7. The mayors seemed to rely only on their political acumen and influence throughout this process. How could senior-level administrative staff be used to assist the mayors in explaining the need for new taxes?

8. How can and should Mayor Myers handle the intergovernmental aspects of this matter? What approaches might he make to Landis to secure its backing? What might he offer to gain some support from the county? How should the intergovernmental contacts be handled? What role, if any, is appropriate for administrative staffs in this effort?

9. Are there other strategies that Mayor Myers might employ? Are there other legitimate tactics that might win support from the other local governing bodies? Are there longer-term strategies that might be pursued, or that the mayor might threaten to pursue, to accomplish his purposes? These strategies might include seeking a change in state laws governing the tax options or seeking to separate Saylor Park from the rest of Fleming County. Be creative in developing new options.

2 Developing the tax base

Editor's introduction

The job of finance administration is not just a matter of balancing revenues and expenditures on a year-by-year basis. While that may be adequate in the short run, the local government administrator, like all public administrators, has a primary responsibility to keep long-run objectives in mind. Often that is not easy, especially if local elected officials seek to maximize in the short run (e.g. until the next election) and let the long run take care of itself.

Nowhere are long-term considerations more important than in financial administration. It is not enough to protect the government from financial scandal or bankruptcy; the competent administrator must strive to ensure that, as the community grows and changes, the funds required to finance essential services and infrastructure improvements will be available when needed. Planning and action are required to develop a tax base that provides enough money to underwrite the services and facilities essential to the community's lifestyle.

This is no small task. It requires a blend of financial expertise and long-range vision; of land and economic development incentives and controls; of managerial, political, and often intergovernmental skills. Frequently, too, the task involves tough, complex ethical choices.

That is the kind of task facing local government management in "Finances and Development." The situation is all too common in large metropolitan areas: a small community with a colorful history, budget problems, and developmental ambitions must improve its financial outlook. Located adjacent to an interstate highway and bordered by unincorporated land, the community must consider both its own long-term financial well-being and the aspirations of a neighboring community also eager to annex land adjacent to the interstate.

Because such land attracts industrial and commercial developments and enriches local tax bases, its annexation promises a financial bonanza for a financially hard-pressed community. But the promise of such a bonanza is attractive to nearby communities as well. The resulting clash of interests could challenge the most skilled diplomat.

In the eye of the storm are the local government manager, finance officer, and development director. They have a professional obligation to optimize the long-term welfare of the community for which they work. They also have an administrative obligation to support the elected officials who employ them.

And so the classic local government management problem is set: the professional staff must use its expertise to formulate recommendations and offer financial analyses of alternative proposals, but such expert vision must be reconciled with political realities. The staff must be cognizant of, and prepared to cope with, political leaders whose behaviors are a product of their individual goals, ambitions, and personalities. Adding to the complexity of this case is the conflict between the community's traditional political culture and its very recent decision to hire professional staff.

At stake is the long-term financial health and well-being of a community that is home to 20,000 people.

Case 2
Finances and development

Bradford J. Townsend

Background

The Village of Oakwood is a small suburban community located within the large metropolitan area of Central City. One of about 340 incorporated suburban municipalities in the metro area, Oakwood lies 35 miles southwest of downtown Central City. It has a population of nearly 20,000 today, but its history can be traced back to a start as a trading post.

The area was inhabited by Native Americans when Clark Lewiston and his expedition explored the Ravine River valley in the 1800s. A settlement named the Town of Oaks was formed as a point of trade along the river. The small town grew modestly and was incorporated in 1901 as the Village of Oakwood, with an at-large village board composed of six trustees and a president, who also held the ceremonial title of mayor. All of the 250 residents lived on the east bank of the Ravine River.

Farming and grain elevator operations were soon added to the base of the economy. The Tri-State Canal and railroad lines, built at about the time of incorporation, greatly increased local commercial activity. In the 1920s, two major oil refineries and a coal-fired electric plant were built. Although one of the refineries closed in later years, others were added and continue in operation today. Nearly all of the original settlement buildings were demolished during a refinery expansion in the 1930s. Several quarries were opened and still furnish the material for roadways and buildings.

Fewer than 800 people lived east of the river in Oakwood when Interstate Highway 62 was built in the 1950s. The new highway ran from a northern point on the Ravine River to a point west and then south away from Oakwood. This placed about ten square miles of farmland in an area north and west of old Oakwood, between the river and the highway (see Figure 1). The village began to annex property in 1955. Annexation accommodated the construction of a new subdivision, known as Oakwood Park, which became a popular choice for residents of the

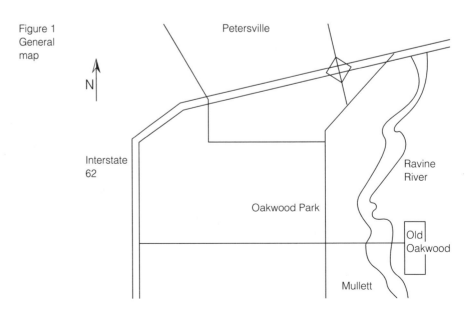

Figure 1
General
map

metropolitan area, especially for first-time homebuyers of modest income and from working-class family backgrounds in Central City. They could buy a prefabricated house with no down payment, a low asking price, and a low mortgage payment. Oakwood experienced a building and population boom that produced a population of 15,000 by 1970.

Residential subdivision development continued but at a slower rate, and the population had grown by fewer than 4,000 residents by the time of the case. The industrial base also continued to grow at a modest rate. The northern geographic boundary of Oakwood reached the Village of Petersville, and the southern boundary was contiguous with the Village of Mullett. Only the highway, farmland, and open space lay to the west.

A tradition of growth

Various mayors and trustees on the Oakwood village board have promoted community growth over the years. The most notable proponent was Dub O'Malley, who served as mayor and board president for more than 35 years. He accommodated the oil companies and the manufactured housing interests that built modern-day Oakwood. One popular story recounts a quickly called meeting in the 1960s to vote for a proposed annexation. The board meeting convened in the old section of town on the east side of the river. Before the vote, O'Malley arranged for the swing bridge over the river to be opened to stop anyone from crossing. The vote was taken, and the meeting was concluded before the detoured objectors arrived.

The death of O'Malley in 1974 prompted the board to create the position of village manager, thus providing for a full-time staff person to administer daily operations while making it difficult for future mayors to hold the same power as O'Malley. The village board continued the growth tradition during this time by purchasing and annexing more property between the river and the highway, even extending this practice to several hundred acres north of Interstate 62 near Petersville. A sanitary sewer main was constructed under the highway to the northern property. This speculative action did not spur development, and the pipeline remained unused. The sewer main did, however, become significant about a decade later.

The case

Among the many people who moved to Oakwood during the O'Malley years was John Wendall. A career high school teacher, Wendall gained his first municipal experience as a part-time director of recreation for Oakwood under O'Malley. He admired O'Malley and learned about politics and finances from the old master. Some years after O'Malley's death, Wendall was elected to two consecutive four-year terms as trustee. Then, three years ago, he decided to run for mayor.

Local unemployment was high because of the closing of two nearby manufacturing plants. Wendall's mayoral campaign message promised to attract new business and industry and to step up the already aggressive annexation activities of the village. Specifically, he promised to push development of vacant properties within the municipal corporate boundary and to expand Oakwood's boundary to include the large tracts of undeveloped farmland to the west. Wendall predicted that his program would reduce residential property taxes because commercial/industrial properties would carry a greater share of the tax burden. He also contended that his efforts would produce more jobs for both white-collar and blue-collar workers.

In addition to the mayor/president position, three of the six trustee positions also were up for election at the same time. Three trustee candidates ran as a team with Wendall. They were all elected and took office with at least a four-person majority. Because the mayor/president could vote in the event of a tie, Wendall and his supporters effectively controlled village policy.

Wendall's first two development initiatives were bold and caused strained relations with neighboring communities. The mayor and board "strip-annexed" industrial property to the north near the boundary with the Village of Petersville. They also convinced a university in the Village of Mullett to de-annex from Mullett and annex to Oakwood in return for utility service. Not surprisingly, these actions angered municipal officials of Petersville and Mullett and created a climate of tough competition for the next round of development initiatives.

Management and finances

Before the election, the incumbent manager had resigned to take another city manager position. Immediately after taking office, the new mayor and a majority of trustees dismissed the replacement manager, who had been on the job about four months, appointing instead the village police chief, who had no general management training or experience.

The new manager's first assignment was to conduct a search for a full-time economic development director. Later that year, he appointed Frank Schmidt, who had worked in the development field for several years in other municipalities and who held an M.P.A. and an M.B.A. degree. Schmidt understood Oakwood's growth tradition and ambition. The board made it clear that it expected development to provide an increased tax base to support municipal services at lower property tax and utility rates for residents. Schmidt proceeded to build on his network of contacts in the development, construction, and real estate fields. He marketed Oakwood as he would a consumer product.

The former-police-chief-turned-manager performed poorly by all accounts. Further, the mayor and board members tended to spend beyond the means of the village. The situation had lasted about a year before the manager was relieved of his duties and retired. Schmidt was assigned the duties of interim village manager while the board conducted a search for a new manager. Considerable financial damage, however, already had been inflicted.

The mayor and trustees hired Dan LeBlanc, who began his new job near the mid-point of Wendall's term of office. He was an experienced local government manager with an M.P.A. degree.

LeBlanc was faced with the dual directive of improving the financial status of the municipal government and promoting economic development. He had discovered before he was hired that the general fund, a few special funds, and the utility enterprise funds were in fair-to-poor condition. His first order of business was to assess the municipal financial status. During the previous two years, the board had overspent by approximately $800,000 in the general fund, and there was no capital fund for utilities.

Table 1 enumerates total budget-to-actual figures for the village's operations during the fiscal year before LeBlanc was hired and for the fiscal year in which he was hired. The fiscal year before LeBlanc was hired is noted on the table as CFY − 3, or three years before the current fiscal year (CFY), the year in which the case events took place. LeBlanc was hired during the second fiscal year before the events in the case, or CFY − 2. Note that, in CFY − 3, actual expenditures of all general fund departments totaled $6.81 million, and revenues were $6.46 million, leaving a deficit of $354,000. CFY − 2 numbers were $6.89 million in expenditures and $6.45 million in revenues, resulting in a $445,000 deficit. Thus, the budget deficit aggregated $799,000 in the two fiscal years preceding the first year for which LeBlanc proposed a village budget.

LeBlanc realized that the financial situation needed to be improved before Oakwood could compete with neighboring villages, Central City, and other municipalities for development. The new manager moved to cut costs, initiating a reduction-in-force of twelve individuals: two firefighters, three public works laborers, and one police records clerk, personnel assistant, secretary, accounting clerk, administrative assistant, planning assistant, and recreation supervisor. This action drew some criticism, but the board members considered it necessary. It represented a savings of over $300,000 annually.

After a survey of the water and sanitary treatment facilities, Manager LeBlanc decided that the infrastructure was in need of capital improvements. He surmised that the Village of Oakwood should not reach out for more territory if it could not adequately meet existing residential, commercial, and industrial needs. The improvements would ensure sufficient service, meet EPA standards, and provide Oakwood with a competitive economic development edge. Improvements included an expansion and effluent discharge modification in the sewage treatment plant, the reacti-

Table 1   Budget-to-actual analysis

	CFY − 3 Budget	CFY − 3 Actual	CFY − 2 Budget	CFY − 2 Actual
Expenditures				
General fund				
Mayor and council	$ 110,000	$ 105,647	$ 111,000	$ 115,233
Clerk	35,000	33,457	35,000	35,666
Manager	187,000	178,888	190,000	189,721
Treasurer	8,000	8,002	9,000	9,216
Legal	150,000	186,611	180,000	206,400
Finance	240,000	233,554	240,000	236,088
Public works	1,000,000	1,103,712	1,000,000	1,133,892
Police	3,200,000	3,199,122	3,200,000	3,201,669
Fire and ambulance	1,550,000	1,606,998	1,550,000	1,610,831
Planning	65,000	65,543	65,000	65,287
Human resources	85,000	87,229	90,000	88,899
Subtotal	$ 6,630,000	$ 6,808,763	$ 6,670,000	$ 6,892,902
Special fund				
Recreation	$ 250,000	$ 223,333	$ 205,000	$ 200,856
Development	400,000	400,000	400,000	325,080
Human relations	120,000	119,876	135,000	129,345
Retirement	500,000	515,610	505,000	523,377
Insurance	300,000	331,005	300,000	335,550
Subtotal	$ 1,570,000	$ 1,589,824	$ 1,545,000	$ 1,514,208
Enterprise fund				
Water utility	$ 2,000,000	$ 2,009,076	$ 2,100,000	$ 2,012,122
Sewage treatment	3,000,000	2,968,820	3,000,000	3,005,664
Subtotal	$ 5,000,000	$ 4,977,896	$ 5,100,000	$ 5,017,786
Total	$13,200,000	$13,376,483	$13,315,000	$13,424,896
Revenues				
Fund				
General	$ 6,630,000	$ 6,455,222	$ 6,670,000	$ 6,448,117
Special	1,570,000	1,605,009	1,570,000	1,520,033
Enterprise	5,000,000	4,977,896	5,100,000	5,199,690
Total	$13,200,000	$13,038,127	$13,340,000	$13,167,840
Annual balance				
Fund				
General	$ 0	$ −353,541	$ 0	$ −444,785
Special	0	15,185	25,000	5,825
Enterprise	0	0	0	181,904

Note: "CFY" refers to current fiscal year. Thus, "CFY − 1"
refers to current fiscal year minus one year. And "CFY −
2" refers to current fiscal year minus two years.

vation of two wells resulting in 1 million more gallons in reserve, and an industrial discharge monitoring project to reduce shock incidents in sewage treatment. Grant dollars were secured, recommendations to increase utility rates and utility taxes were approved, and the manager's conservative budget proposals were adopted.

Table 2 shows total budget-to-actual figures for the first two years in which LeBlanc was responsible for budget development and implementation: the current fiscal year (CFY) and the previous year (CFY − 1). Note that in CFY − 1, actual expenditures for all general fund departments totaled $6.60 million and that revenues were $6.51 million, leaving a deficit of about $99,000. Current fiscal year

Table 2 Budget-to-actual analysis	CFY − 1 Budget	CFY − 1 Actual	CFY Budget
Expenditures			
General fund			
Mayor and council	$ 100,000	$ 99,300	$ 100,000
Clerk	33,000	30,005	33,000
Manager	175,000	173,381	175,000
Treasurer	9,000	8,884	9,000
Legal	200,000	203,398	185,000
Finance	240,000	220,556	220,000
Public works	980,000	978,660	980,000
Police	3,190,000	3,192,283	3,190,000
Fire and ambulance	1,600,000	1,597,616	1,600,000
Planning	35,000	34,422	35,000
Human resources	70,000	65,558	70,000
Subtotal	$ 6,632,000	$ 6,604,063	$ 6,597,000
Special fund			
Tax increment	$ 150,000	$ 75,555	$ 200,000
Recreation	200,000	176,486	180,000
Development	330,000	324,390	440,000
Human relations	125,000	122,345	125,000
Retirement	500,000	502,363	505,000
Insurance	315,000	315,000	315,000
Subtotal	$ 1,620,000	$ 1,516,139	$ 1,765,000
Enterprise fund			
Water utility	$ 2,000,000	$ 2,009,076	$ 2,225,000
Sewage treatment	3,000,000	2,968,820	3,850,000
Subtotal	5,000,000	4,977,896	6,075,000
Total	$ 3,252,000	$13,098,098	$14,437,000
Revenues			
Fund			
General	$ 6,632,000	$ 6,505,222	$ 6,597,000
Special	1,620,000	1,605,009	1,765,000
Enterprise	5,000,000	4,977,896	6,075,000
Total	$13,252,000	$13,088,127	$14,437,000
Annual balance			
Fund			
General	$ 0	$ −98,841	$ 0
Special	0	88,870	0
Enterprise	0	0	0

Note: "CFY" refers to current fiscal year. Thus, "CFY − 1"
  refers to current fiscal year minus one year.

(CFY) numbers predict $6.60 million in expenditures and $6.60 million in revenues, or a balanced budget. The two-year deficit would thus be $99,000, down by over 800 percent from the previous two years.

Other players in the case

Besides LeBlanc and Schmidt, the other staff support persons involved in financial and development matters included the finance director, village engineer, and village attorney. The engineer was on contract and had more than two decades of civil engineering experience. The finance director had limited formal education but some practical experience in office accounting. Both confined their activities to technical advice and information gathering.

The village attorney, however, played a much broader role. Bill Ewing was appointed by the board to be the municipal legal counsel shortly after Wendall was elected mayor. Ewing was a longtime political ally of Mayor Wendall and had served as chairman of the county board for several years. Although he was officially retained to provide legal counsel to village officials, his primary informal duty was to enhance John Wendall's political career. Ewing helped negotiate and draft agreements with developers, an expected practice for a municipal legal counsel, but his approach to that activity became a point of contention among the professional staff.

Development initiatives

Economic Development Director Schmidt moved forward on several growth initiatives. He developed marketing packages to lure developers, businesspeople, and builders. The packages highlighted the improved water and sewer utility services that could be provided to suitable unincorporated land adjacent to the village.

Economically depressed properties within the municipal boundary were targeted. Acting on Schmidt's recommendation, with Manager LeBlanc's concurrence, the village board designated one area to be a tax increment financing district and another to be an enterprise zone.

The purpose of the tax increment financing (TIF) district is to promote development by creating a financing mechanism to pay for infrastructure improvements that otherwise would not be feasible in economically depressed areas. Money for such improvements is raised through bond issues, which then are repaid by increments in property tax receipts in the affected district. Presumably, the improvements attract new development, which in turn is the source of the tax increments. Existing units of government, such as the schools and the county, do not receive any of the tax increment dollars until the bonds have been paid off. The increase in the tax base is expected to provide jobs immediately and additional revenues to all local governments in the area at a later date.

The purpose of the enterprise zone is to spur economic development by reducing taxes and fees on business and industry willing to locate in the zone. Incentives may include a reduction or waiver of taxes on sales and property. Fees commonly reduced or waived relate to subdivision plans, building codes, and zoning codes. The ultimate goal is to generate new jobs from the attraction or expansion of business or industry.

The village began to receive a major response to its new development overtures two years ago. Among the proposals were two new residential subdivisions, two residential subdivision expansions, three new business parks, two new industrial parks, a religious convention center, and an airport expansion. Building permit applications were filed for a yearly record of over 500,000 square feet of new construction last year.

Three of the development projects became the subjects of substantial study and negotiation. They included a residential subdivision, a business park on property owned by the village, and another business park near the Petersville border. The first two depended upon the construction of an interchange on I-62. All three needed municipal water and sewer utilities. The level of planning activity placed a heavy strain on the time, skill, and resources of the staff and board.

A tale of two cities and three developments

Sunmore Corporation of Florida proposed a residential development for "active adults" on 1,200 acres of farmland in the western area between Oakwood and the highway. The units would be townhouses, condominiums, and apartments. A golf course and recreation center would be built on-site, and access would be controlled by a gatekeeper. The preliminary plan called for residential development in 15 phases, resulting in 10,000 residents at total buildout. The concept revolved around the notion that some retirees would stay in the Midwest, rather than move south, if suitable housing of this kind were available.

The Sunmore corporate leaders wanted to connect to the Oakwood water and sewer service, which would be a less costly and quicker option for them than starting a new utility operation. It might have been possible to build a well-based water system on-site, but there was no point of discharge next to the property for treated wastewater.

Sunmore officials also wanted The Hamptons, as the development would be called, to remain unincorporated, allowing the development to retain its own identity during marketing efforts, to stay at arm's length from the Oakwood reputation for starter housing, and to permit construction under a less restrictive county building code. The developers also wanted an interstate interchange built adjacent to the site.

Meanwhile, BIG Development Corporation of California proposed a 450-acre business park on property north of I-62 that the village had bought in the previous decade. The land lay about one-half mile north of the proposed site for The Hamptons. BIG corporate officers planned to construct steel-frame buildings for businesses that required ready access to the highway transportation system. They had succeeded in the past by placing business parks next to existing or new interchanges. BIG also developed those properties by applying the planned unit development (PUD) method to the business park environment, thus gaining maximum flexibility in developing the property. Utilities would be provided to the site through the old sanitary sewer line constructed under the interstate ten years earlier, and the proposed business park would be named Continental Center.

The need for an interchange was the primary common denominator for both major projects. Mayor Wendall proceeded to work with the governor's office and state legislators, while Manager LeBlanc contacted officials of the state departments of transportation and economic development. The heads of Sunmore and BIG were brought into the effort to push for the project. The interchange project was approved after much lobbying, cost-benefit analysis, a preliminary engineering study, and other activities.

Financing for the interchange amounted to a leverage of municipal funds to gain state and developer contributions for the project. The total budget was $14.5 million. The respective participation became as follows: Oakwood, $3 million; Sunmore, $1.5 million; BIG, $1.5 million; and the state, $8.5 million. The Oakwood share was derived from the sale of the northern property to BIG. The county already had contributed in the form of a major road, running next to the Sunmore and BIG properties, that would serve as the interchange cross-road for ingress and egress.

The Hamptons and the Continental Center project began independently but became intertwined because of the mutual need for the proposed highway interchange. A third project started separately as well but became intertwined for a different reason. Tennison Incorporated of New York began looking at property in the Oakwood-Petersville area on which to develop a business park. It talked with numerous local property owners and decided to work with Al Rothman, a developer/speculator and the owner of property throughout the metropolitan area. Most of the time, he acted purely as a speculator. He would buy property and try to sell or "flip" it as soon as possible. The actual development would be carried out by others.

In concert with Tennison, Rothman tried to "play-off" Petersville against Oakwood in an effort to obtain the best incentive deal. Tennison prepared a development plan for a 350-acre parcel of property that would become a combination business and industrial park with large warehousing facilities and would be named Southwest Business Park.

At this point, the mayor of Petersville, Lyle Quayle, became a prominent figure in Oakwood development projects. He was the elected leader of a community with nearly 40,000 residents and an annual budget nearly twice the size of Oakwood's: $26 million versus $14 million. Quayle was well connected with the governor and other influential members of the state's administration. He was also a member of the inner circle that headed the prevailing political party of the county. He held a Ph.D. degree and was the president of a local business college. Quayle and his colleagues on the Petersville Board of Trustees were also development-minded; they had worked for many years to promote residential and commercial development. The new I-62 interchange was viewed by Quayle as an opportunity to "piggyback" on the success of Oakwood officials to achieve more gains for Petersville.

Mayors Quayle and Wendall ostensibly were competitors as the chief elected officers of their respective municipalities. At the same time, they were members of the same political clique in the county. It was this connection that led Quayle and Wendall to begin talking informally about possible ways to deal jointly with developers and property owners. The two agreed that Rothman and Tennison were only the most recent in a series of developers who had attempted the "play-off" tactic.

Wendall knew that rival Petersville had more resources to offer financial incentives. Quayle knew that rival Oakwood had superior water and sewer resources. They decided that the formation of a boundary-line agreement was the answer. Such an arrangement between municipalities, as specifically authorized by the state constitution and statutes, could provide for the sharing of limited resources and designate territories for annexation in advance. Neither municipality had such an agreement with any other community. The mayors went back to their respective boards and staffs to begin a boundary-line negotiation process.

Staff advice and politics don't mix

In Oakwood, LeBlanc and Schmidt began a study of boundary-line issues at the board's request. The two staff professionals conducted a cost-benefit analysis. Cost factors included new services, capital improvements, used utility capacity, shared revenues, and the effects of the TIF district and enterprise zone. Benefit factors encompassed new taxes, new fees, new infrastructure, and new jobs.

LeBlanc and Schmidt recommended that the boundary should run along a line roughly parallel to I-62. (See Figure 2. Note that the proposed agreement basically reserved future annexation to Oakwood south of the highway and to Petersville north of the highway.) The two officials pointed to the considerable leverage that Oakwood had, thanks to the strong water supply/transmission main and substantial sewer capacity to meet utility demands for new developments. They also acknowledged that Petersville had considerable resources. Nevertheless, it would be nearly impossible for that municipality to extend its utility lines south of I-62 due to engineering problems and a contract with an investor-owned utility. The respective mayors, attorneys, and managers took part in the early negotiating sessions, which made some minor modifications to the map.

About two-thirds of the way through the process, Wendall and Ewing decided to change the negotiation strategy and approached Quayle directly. The sessions became off-limits to the managers and staff of both communities. Final negotiating sessions involved only the two mayors, with background support from their respective lawyers. The managers of both communities expressed concerns about the

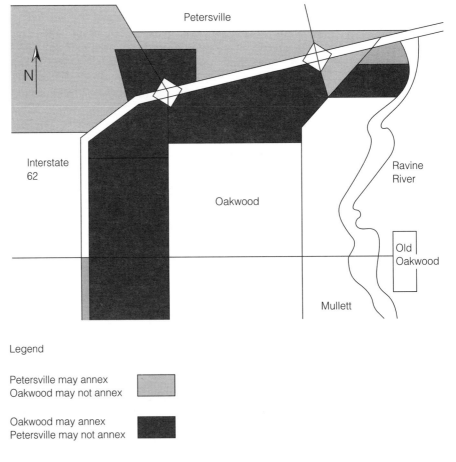

Figure 2 Oakwood/
Petersville boundary-line
agreement proposed by
LeBlanc and Schmidt

Legend

Petersville may annex
Oakwood may not annex

Oakwood may annex
Petersville may not annex

proposed agreement to their respective boards in executive session but had no
influence. LeBlanc felt that Wendall had mistakenly assumed that he and Schmidt
were opposed to the agreement; also, he was worried about Quayle's ability to run
circles around Wendall.

The final draft of a boundary-line agreement was prepared, focusing on the I-62
area generally. It would control where and under what circumstances annexation
would occur over the next twenty years. Southwest Business Park, The Hamptons,
and Continental Center all figured in the document. Southwest Business Park would
be located on land south of the highway and be contiguous to both villages. The
property would be annexed to Petersville, but the two villages would share any tax
revenue. Oakwood would provide utilities at its own cost and derive all income
from the rates charged. (See Figure 3. Note that the boundary had changed con-
siderably from the original staff proposal. Also, the Village of Petersville had at-
tained considerable gains in the joint acreage.)

LeBlanc and the Oakwood staff ran a final cost-benefit analysis on the Southwest
Business Park proposal. The manager told Wendall that the project was a marginal-
to-poor deal for Oakwood and was in effect a ''gift'' to Petersville. LeBlanc was
concerned about the ability of the village to finance utility improvements at the
five- and ten-year marks. Further, he complained that the joint property tax clause
in the agreement was lopsided in favor of Petersville. Concerning the boundary-
line provisions, he pointed to the large acreage south of I-62 that Oakwood would
be prohibited from annexing. Much of it was already contiguous to Oakwood but
not to Petersville. Another objection was the clause allowing Petersville the right
to annex one of the quadrants around the new interchange, even though Petersville
would have contributed nothing to that project.

Figure 3 Oakwood/
Petersville boundary-line
agreement proposed by
Wendall and Ewing

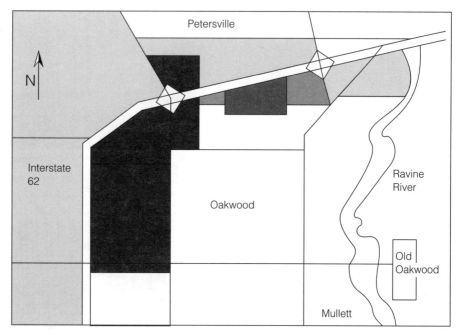

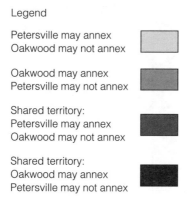

Legend

Petersville may annex
Oakwood may not annex

Oakwood may annex
Petersville may not annex

Shared territory:
Petersville may annex
Oakwood may not annex

Shared territory:
Oakwood may annex
Petersville may not annex

LeBlanc voiced the same concerns privately to the board. He said that it should still consider an agreement with more favorable provisions for Oakwood. (Table 3 is the cost-benefit analysis spreadsheet developed by the staff. It compared benefits and costs for the Wendall-Ewing plan, shown in Figure 3, with those of the Le-Blanc-Schmidt plan, shown in Figure 2.)

The cost-benefit analysis clearly indicated that both plans eventually would have a positive net result for Oakwood. However, the LeBlanc-Schmidt plan would be $9.1 million better over twenty years for Oakwood. It provided for police and fire service responsibilities to be shared more equitably between Oakwood and Petersville. As shown in Table 3, costs for Oakwood police protection, fire prevention, and construction of fire stations over twenty years total $6.1 million under the Wendall-Ewing plan and $3.55 million under the LeBlanc-Schmidt proposal. Further, the LeBlanc-Schmidt proposal contained a formula that more equitably apportioned the revenues to be shared by the two municipalities. Property tax and utility charge income figures over twenty years were projected at $17.38 million for Oakwood under the Wendall-Ewing plan and $23.15 million under LeBlanc-Schmidt. The Wendall-Ewing plan was more expensive for Oakwood because it shifted a greater burden of providing ongoing police and fire services onto Oak-

(*continued on page 24*)

Table 3   Cost-benefit analysis spreadsheet

Cost-benefit analysis for Oakwood/Petersville boundary-line agreement (Wendall-Ewing plan)

Item	CFY	CFY + 1	CFY + 2	CFY + 3	CFY + 4	CFYs + 5 to + 20	Totals
Water tower/lines	$ −225,000	$ −225,000	$ −225,000	$ −225,000	$ −225,000	$ −850,000	$ −1,975,000
Sanitary sewer line	−120,000	−120,000	−120,000	−120,000	−120,000	−400,000	−1,000,000
Sewage capacity ($ value)	−300,000	−200,000	−400,000	−300,000	−200,000	−100,000	−1,500,000
Storm sewers	−50,000	−100,000	−75,000	−50,000	−100,000	−300,000	−675,000
Police protection	−50,000	−50,000	−50,000	−50,000	−50,000	−750,000	−1,000,000
Fire prevention	−200,000	−200,000	−200,000	−200,000	−200,000	−3,000,000	−4,000,000
Fire stations (2)	−200,000	−200,000	−200,000	−200,000	−300,000		−1,100,000
Road construction	−100,000	−100,000	−100,000	−100,000	−100,000	−500,000	−1,000,000
Road maintenance/snow plow	−100,000	−150,000	−200,000	−250,000	−300,000	−4,500,000	−5,500,000
Interest on debt	−50,000	−100,000	−100,000	−100,000	−150,000	−1,100,000	−1,600,000
Total costs	$−1,395,000	$−1,445,000	$−1,670,000	$−1,595,000	$−1,745,000	$−11,500,000	$−19,350,000
Property tax	$ 35,000	$ 35,000	$ 35,000	$ 175,000	$ 200,000	$ 3,000,000	$ 3,480,000
Income/sales tax	50,000	75,000	100,000	175,000	300,000	5,000,000	5,700,000
Miscellaneous fees	30,000	30,000	20,000	20,000	100,000	500,000	700,000
Utility charges	400,000	450,000	500,000	500,000	850,000	11,200,000	13,900,000
Jobs ($ value new)	200,000	400,000	450,000	300,000	200,000	1,000,000	2,550,000
Total benefits	$ 715,000	$ 990,000	$ 1,105,000	$ 1,170,000	$ 1,650,000	$ 20,700,000	$ 26,330,000
Net result	$ −680,000	$ −455,000	$ −565,000	$ −425,000	$ −95,000	$ 9,200,000	$ 6,980,000

Cost-benefit analysis for
Oakwood/Petersville boundary-line agreement
(LeBlanc-Schmidt proposal)

Item	CFY	CFY + 1	CFY + 2	CFY + 3	CFY + 4	CFYs + 5 to + 20	Totals
Water tower/lines	$ −225,000	$ −225,000	$ −225,000	$ −225,000	$ −225,000	$ −850,000	$ −1,975,000
Sanitary sewer line	−120,000	−120,000	−120,000	−120,000	−120,000	−400,000	−1,000,000
Sewage capacity ($ value)	−300,000	−200,000	−400,000	−300,000	−200,000	−100,000	−1,500,000
Storm sewers	−50,000	−100,000	−75,000	−50,000	−100,000	−300,000	−675,000
Police protection	−30,000	−30,000	−30,000	−30,000	−30,000	−450,000	−600,000
Fire prevention	−120,000	−120,000	−120,000	−120,000	−120,000	−1,800,000	−2,400,000
Fire station	−100,000	−100,000	−100,000	−100,000	−150,000		−550,000
Road construction	−100,000	−100,000	−100,000	−100,000	−100,000	−500,000	−1,000,000
Road maintenance/snow plow	−100,000	−150,000	−200,000	−250,000	−300,000	−4,500,000	−5,500,000
Interest on debt	−50,000	−100,000	−100,000	−100,000	−100,000	−700,000	−1,150,000
Total costs	$ −1,195,000	$ −1,245,000	$ −1,470,000	$ −1,395,000	$ −1,445,000	$ −9,600,000	$ −16,350,000
Property tax	$ 50,000	$ 50,000	$ 50,000	$ 200,000	$ 250,000	$ 3,750,000	$ 4,350,000
Income/sales tax	50,000	75,000	100,000	175,000	300,000	5,000,000	5,700,000
Miscellaneous fees	30,000	30,000	20,000	20,000	150,000	750,000	1,000,000
Utility charges	500,000	600,000	800,000	900,000	1,000,000	15,000,000	18,800,000
Jobs ($ value new)	200,000	400,000	450,000	300,000	200,000	1,000,000	2,550,000
Total benefits	$ 830,000	$ 1,155,000	$ 1,420,000	$ 1,595,000	$ 1,900,000	$ 25,500,000	$ 32,400,000
Net result	$ −365,000	$ −90,000	$ −50,000	$ 200,000	$ 455,000	$ 15,900,000	$ 16,050,000

Note: "CFY" refers to current fiscal year. Thus, "CFY + 1 (... + 5)" refers to current fiscal year plus one (or five) year(s).

wood. The LeBlanc-Schmidt proposal was more beneficial because it channeled a substantially larger revenue stream to Oakwood.

LeBlanc and a financial consultant studied alternative cash flow projections. They determined that a joint long-term revenue bond and a joint general obligation bond were feasible. However, LeBlanc was concerned about the negative cost-benefit numbers during the first five years of the Wendall-Ewing plan and the first three years of the LeBlanc-Schmidt proposal. It was determined that the bonds could be structured to schedule lower installment payments during the early years. However, LeBlanc told the mayor and trustees that there was a real possibility of default during years six through twelve under Wendall-Ewing. LeBlanc believed that plan posed an unnecessary financial risk to the village.

LeBlanc cited the cost-benefit analysis as a reason to recommend the proposal that he developed with the assistance of Schmidt and others on the staff. Wendall still supported the boundary-line document that he and Ewing had negotiated with Quayle. The mayor planned to ask the village board to vote for approval on September 28. Wendall and Leblanc met alone in the mayor's office that afternoon. The mayor expressed his displeasure at the negative assessment that the manager had offered to him and other members of the board. He advised LeBlanc either to speak in favor of the Wendall-Ewing plan or to "shut up" during the board meeting.

The decision problem

LeBlanc felt as if he had been on a roller coaster for two years. A substantial amount of professional work had gone into operational, capital, and economic development activities since he had come to Oakwood. He and others could point to an impressive list of accomplishments. He did not want to see these accomplishments squandered by a boundary-line agreement based upon poor economics and questionable politics. He was concerned about the risk and the potential negative impact on the citizens of Oakwood. As he prepared for the village board meeting, he carefully considered the mayor's ultimatum and identified the following alternative courses of action:

> Stay with the staff's cost-benefit numbers in hand (Table 3). Present them in a matter-of-fact manner at the meeting.

> Revise the assumptions in the cost-benefit analysis. Raise the projections of potential benefits in terms of tax revenue and utility rate income. Lower to the extreme the estimated cost of infrastructure improvements.

> Take the mayor's advice and "shut up." Let the economic development director or finance director present the staff position.

> Stay with the cost-benefit numbers in hand. Express concern openly about the numbers and the risk to the village.

LeBlanc had just a few hours to decide on his course of action.

Discussion questions

1. Has LeBlanc fulfilled his duty by advising the mayor and board members privately? Why or why not?
2. Can LeBlanc be convincing or engender confidence in the proposed boundary-line agreement with a matter-of-fact presentation at the board meeting? What probably will happen if he is questioned extensively?
3. Consider the probable consequences if the manager revises the cost-benefit analysis with rosy numbers. What revisions can he make? What are the risks

to the community? What are the ethical problems for LeBlanc? What could be the impact on financial gains achieved in the last fiscal year and this fiscal year?

4. Is it feasible for the manager to remain silent and let others speak? Would inaction speak louder than words? Should he consider not attending the session? Why or why not?

5. LeBlanc was frustrated by the fact that he was excluded from the final boundary-line negotiations. What could he have done to maintain involvement? Could he have provided any financial information earlier in the process, or in a different way, to influence the participants? How far does his professional obligation to protect the well-being of the community permit him to go in his attempts to influence the mayor's behavior?

6. Are there other strategies that LeBlanc should consider? If so, what are they? What would be their likely consequences?

7. Does the boundary-line disagreement between Wendall and LeBlanc indicate a more fundamental problem with board-manager relations in Oakwood? If so, define it.

8. What should LeBlanc do? Why?

3 Estimating revenues

Editor's introduction

The typical federal or state administrator starts the budget preparation process by reviewing guidelines from the budget office for the year under consideration. Those guidelines articulate executive policies for the forthcoming budget year and describe parameters within which the administrator's budget requests should be contained. The guidelines may or may not make any references to estimated revenues; revenue estimates for future years are made by the central budget office, not by the agency administrator.

This is not true for the manager or finance officer of a city or county government. For them, the budget preparation process starts with the job of estimating revenues. Indeed, their whole financial planning process requires, and depends on, high-quality revenue estimates, not just to prepare next year's operating budget, but also to formulate the multi-year capital budget and, as the previous two cases demonstrated, to guide long-term planning and economic development efforts. Unlike their federal or state counterparts, then, local government administrators must know and understand the methodologies involved in estimating revenues.

At first glance, those methodologies might appear simple, if any task involving the application of statistics can be described as simple. They require the collection of current data, much of which is compiled and can be obtained from others, and the analysis of that data through the application of standard statistical formulas and computer programs. The fewer the changes made in the process each year, the more comparable the data will be from year to year and thus the easier it will be for those doing the estimation to assess trends and make projections over time.

Yet, as the case ''Forecasting in Timber City'' demonstrates vividly, the process is anything but simple. Changes in laws, intergovernmental revenues, the economy, and the community occur constantly, and such changes affect revenues, often in ways that are hard to predict. But even more, the process is complicated by the need to make assumptions: assumptions about data, especially when the data are not compiled in comparable ways or reported for comparable time frames; assumptions about adjustments for missing or unavailable data; assumptions involved in the choice of alternative statistical/analytical techniques; assumptions about the secondary and tertiary effects—the multiplier effects—of forecasted changes; even assumptions about how people, businesses, and the economy will respond to predicted changes.

Perhaps most difficult of all is the policy choice regarding the assumptions. Should assumptions be designed to produce conservative estimates? To protect themselves, many administrators prefer to make conservative estimates of revenues and liberal estimates of expenditures, thereby assuring their city or county of financial health in most worse-case scenarios. But, as this case suggests, conservative estimates lead to reductions in service and personnel and have a real effect on people's jobs and lives. Decisions with this kind of impact are never easy.

This case also provides insight into another dynamic of the administrative process: the interaction of the administrator with outside consultants. Managers and their staffs cannot have expertise in all fields. For specialized tasks, such as the sophisticated revenue projections required in this case, they frequently call on the expertise of outsiders—consultants. But the delineation of the charge to the consultants, and the subsequent need to guide and apply their results, are themselves difficult.

Ultimately, as Manager O'Reilly in Timber City realizes, the completion of sophisticated analyses does not resolve political quandaries. Hard decisions still need to be made; the realities uncovered by the consultants still need to be reconciled with the perceptions of the politicians. While the administrator can draw heavily on the "science" of public administration to answer technical questions, the "art" of administration—the need to deal with people and politics—still must be addressed.

The job of applying the "art" in public administration, the need to accommodate empirical knowledge with the political inclinations of others, is the loneliest, hardest task in the management of local government.

Case 3
Forecasting in Timber City
Jon S. Ebeling, Frederica Shockley, and William A. Murphy

Background

Timber City, whose population is 8,700, is a timber-dependent community in Bunyan County, in the northeastern part of the state. Timber City is adjacent to a larger city (population of 80,000) that serves as the region's retail trading center. While the larger city attracts most of the retail activity, Timber City and its environs have a number of mills employing several thousand workers; these include several large sawmills (the largest of which employs 370) and a large paper mill with a separate pulp mill.

A nationwide recession currently is having a serious effect on the state economy, although so far the impact has been greatest in the southern part of the state. Locally, however, the timber industry faces a sharp reduction in the supply of logs. Officials concerned about the general economic uncertainty and the local dependence on the timber industry have taken a number of steps to diversify the city's revenue base. For example, to take advantage of the interstate highway that runs through Timber City, City Manager Neil O'Reilly and other leaders have pursued an economic development strategy encouraging highway-supported businesses. The results have included a 160,000-square-foot factory outlet shopping center adjacent to the interstate, a regional furniture store, and a motel. During the past five years, these operations have attracted fast-food outlets and other highway-dependent businesses.

During the past summer, local businesses had seemed to be doing pretty well, and there was no talk of layoffs. Thus, when a series of economic problems surfaced, the city manager and the council were taken by surprise. First, construction of a 140-unit subdivision—which Timber City staff had expected to be rapidly completed—stopped suddenly, and the builder filed for bankruptcy. Then, several other developers postponed construction of developments that already had been approved by the city planning department, and revenue from building permits fell below estimates.

Although sales-tax receipts, now the predominant source of general fund revenue, had not yet begun to show signs of decline, the owners of the factory outlet center reported that sales were not meeting their expectations. Something was wrong, but it was not clear what was causing the problem or how serious it was.

City staff members are not privy to all the financial problems of local businesses, let alone those of the corporations that own and operate the mills. Autumn brought a chill to city officials when one of the larger sawmills announced that mill operations would cease in sixty days, leaving 328 employees out of work. It was clear that the loss of jobs and commercial activity would have a significant impact on the community, but precisely what the impact would be on Timber City's budget —and especially on tax revenues—was uncertain.

The case

Even before the announcement of the mill closing, Manager O'Reilly had anticipated impending problems and asked the finance department to analyze the city's financial status. The report indicated that the general fund probably would lose revenue from several sources: First, the state was improving its own general fund by reclaiming revenue that previously had been transferred to local agencies. (Earlier changes in the state law already had caused Timber City to lose portions of traffic safety fines and cigarette taxes.) Second, new laws required Timber City to pay fees to the county for jail bookings and for administering the property tax. Third, the state had changed the allocation formula for the distribution of property tax revenue, causing a drop of more than $50,000 in Timber City's revenues. According to the finance department report, if existing service levels were maintained, this combination of revenue reductions and new required expenditures probably would lead to a $160,000 shortfall in the general fund for the coming fiscal year.

The report suggested that, as a new source of revenue to the city, the factory outlet center had masked the impact of the recession. Manager O'Reilly already knew that the center's owners were complaining that sales had been lower than expected. Putting together the information gleaned from the report and his own knowledge of the local economy, Manager O'Reilly realized that he probably had overestimated sales-tax proceeds for the current year, as would become apparent when fourth-quarter sales were reported in the following March. Table 1 indicates recent trends in city revenue sources.

As he read the report, O'Reilly realized that Timber City finally was facing the impact of the national recession. Because income falls during a recession, revenues derived from consumption expenditures—such as sales and use taxes and motor vehicle license fees—also decline. Declining construction activity reduces revenues from building permits and other fees. Although the city's revenue-producing economic development efforts had succeeded in maintaining adequate general fund

Table 1   Timber City revenue trend (in dollars)

	CFY*	% of total	CFY − 1	% of total	CFY − 2	% of total	CFY − 3	% of total
Revenue sources								
Property	$ 602,000	12.1	$ 634,821	9.9	$ 769,619	15.2	$ 425,389	10.1
Sales	1,011,528	20.3	931,398	14.6	781,478	15.5	685,513	16.3
Utility users/licenses	227,377	4.5	216,060	3.4	189,944	3.8	376,073	9.0
Permits, fines	447,014	9.0	559,876	8.8	452,616	9.0	415,121	9.9
IGR revenue	1,092,721	21.9	1,724,574	27.0	1,270,446	25.2	1,107,901	26.4
Service charges	1,521,514	30.5	1,839,917	28.8	1,459,515	28.9	1,089,983	25.9
Other revenue	87,861	1.8	479,842	7.5	123,370	2.4	101,633	2.4
Total revenue	$4,990,015	100.0	$6,386,488	100.0	$5,046,988	100.0	$4,201,613	100.0

*"CFY" refers to current fiscal year.

reserves, they had provided only a temporary buffer against the economic woes that eventually might make their way north from the southern part of the state.

After reading the report, O'Reilly decided to reduce expenditures where possible during the current year. Most significant, he postponed hiring two replacement police officers until the financial situation had become clearer.

As Manager O'Reilly looked at the data in Table 1, he noticed the rapid increase in the proportion of general fund revenues coming from the sales tax. Now confronted with the mill closure as well, O'Reilly knew that the community faced serious cutbacks in service levels. Particularly, he was concerned about cutbacks because some city departments were staffed by only one person: layoffs would eliminate some services entirely.

O'Reilly knew that the statewide recession already was affecting the city's revenue, primarily through the loss of state assistance. The plant closing would bring an additional impact, not only through the loss of in-plant and plant-related jobs but also through the reduction in sales-tax revenue. The impact on the real estate market would depend on how many of the plant employees actually lived in Timber City. O'Reilly needed to know what changes to expect in city revenues: the Timber City Economic Development Committee and the city council wanted an analysis.

The manager also was confronted with a number of related questions:

1.   How many jobs, in addition to those cut at the mill, will be lost after the mill closes? In other words, what will be the multiplier effect of the mill closing be?
2.   What will be the impact of the mill closing on Timber City's budget?
3.   In what other ways might the mill closure affect the region's economy?
4.   How can the impact of the state's economic recession be separated from the impact of the mill closure on the local economy?
5.   What steps should the council take to maintain a "reasonably" balanced budget? Increase revenues? Cut services? Draw on reserves?

Answers to these questions would come, in part, from the findings of the economic analysis required to develop good revenue projections.

Forecasting methods

Timber City staff traditionally had made revenue projections on the basis of the state's estimates, with adjustments derived from their knowledge of local trends, new businesses, and loss of businesses. Although it was not a rigorous approach, it was adequate as long as a growing economy drove revenues up.

Now that the situation abruptly had become more complex, Manager O'Reilly felt that he needed to take a more sophisticated approach to revenue projection. He contacted two consultants, Robert and Eve Smith, and explained that he needed a forecast of his sales-tax revenues over the next two years—with and without the mill closure.

After Manager O'Reilly had filled them in on the background, the Smiths suggested that the best approach would be to use linear regression analysis, a statistical technique for determining relationships among data series over time. The Smiths explained that when regression analysis shows a strong relationship between two variables over time, this relationship could be used to make short-term predictions for the future. To examine the impact of the mill closure, Robert and Eve said that they would use IMPLAN, an input-output model developed to analyze the economic impact of changes such as mill closures.[1] Data would come from the annual reports produced by the state's board of equalization, which contain annual sales-tax revenue estimates for all counties and cities in the state.

Robert and Eve also explained that they already had data for Bunyan County that they used with IMPLAN. Although they would have to work with county-level data to determine the impact of the mill closure, the Smiths assured Manager

O'Reilly that they could use the results to adjust their forecasts of city sales-tax revenues. Clearly interested, O'Reilly pressed the consultants for more details.

"First, we'll use regression analysis to estimate the relationship between taxable sales and personal income," Robert explained.

"What does that mean?" O'Reilly asked. "Look, these folks on the council need to communicate with citizens. We can't get involved in teaching a statistics course."

"Don't be concerned. We'll explain all of our results in simple terms. We'll use input-output analysis to determine the potential impact of the mill's closure on output, income, and jobs; then, we'll use the forecasted change in income to estimate the impact of the mill's closure on taxable sales," Eve continued.

Manager O'Reilly was intrigued, but he was concerned about a couple of other problems; one was the revenue from the shopping center, and the other a recently instituted snack tax. Although O'Reilly knew that the snack tax would contribute to Timber City's revenues, he did not know by how much. Moreover, he suspected that the revenue increase would be short-lived: public outcry against the tax probably would lead to its repeal. "How will you forecast the revenue from our shopping center? What about the snack tax? I need to know what will happen if it stays in place—*and* what will happen if it's repealed," O'Reilly said.

Robert explained that the state government had spent heavily to build professional expertise in financial forecasting over the years, and that the state commission on finance produced not only its own state budget forecasts but also a highly sophisticated and respected set of data on the state's economy. "I'm sure that the state commission on finance will have some estimates on the impact of the snack tax," Robert continued. "And maybe we can find some data from other sources to estimate the sales at your shopping center."

"We'll fax you a proposal tomorrow," Eve added.

Data collection

Before the ink could dry on the contract, the Smiths began collecting data. They obtained annual data for Timber City's total taxable transactions from the state board of equalization's (BOE) publications for the past fifteen years. Robert and Eve also asked Manager O'Reilly's office to provide data on sales-tax revenues; city staff forwarded copies of the quarterly reports they received from BOE's division of local government allocation.

Robert, always skeptical of data, compared the figures he had obtained from the state with those from Timber City. Much to his dismay, he found that the amount reported to the city by the BOE was greater than the amount reported by the state in its annual reports. He immediately called the BOE about the discrepancy. When staff members in the state office could not explain the difference, Robert asked Manager O'Reilly about it. O'Reilly was surprised to learn that his records showed more sales-tax revenue than the state's reports. Although he had no explanation, he assured the consultants that the state's division of local government allocation had never bounced a check.

Robert was frustrated: "I can't use the city's data because they're quarterly by fiscal year, and all of the other data are based on annual calendar years. Not only that, but we're going back twenty years, and some of the city's quarterly reports are missing. But I can't use the state's data either, because they would underestimate the amount the city receives."

Robert started making phone calls. He needed annual population data for Timber City, and he needed to clarify the discrepancy between the BOE's annual data and the quarterly reports it had sent to the city. Robert had the data from the various decennial censuses of Timber City: the problem was estimating population during the intermediate years. He called the Timber City finance office and found that it had some population data but that these findings had not been collected systematically. Timber City staff had figures for some years, and the state department of finance had figures for others, but there were still some periods missing—four years, to be exact. "Well," Robert thought, "the best thing to do is to take the average annual population change from the prior three years, average those values, and then use the resulting figure to fill in the missing information."

The problem of the discrepancy between the two BOE reports was more perplexing. Robert called the BOE and spoke with Elaine Morrison, the agency's data specialist for local government. She assured him that the annual data were correct. He hung up and thought for a moment, wondering whether the discrepancy came from the timing of the reporting cycles.

When Robert called back, Elaine connected him with her supervisor, Bill Mackler, who immediately explained the problem: the difference was caused by the fact that the Timber City data included accounts receivable and statewide and countywide "pooled revenue money." Mackler explained that some firms that sell statewide have home offices in various counties; the sales tax from these firms must be distributed through a complex formula to all 458 cities and 58 counties.

When Robert asked him what the average difference was, Mackler said, "Oh, about 12 percent." Skeptical as ever, Robert asked one of his graduate students to go over the data to double-check Mackler's figure. When the student confirmed the 12 percent differential, Robert felt confident in deciding to use the annual state data and then to adjust his results upward to account for the average difference between the two series.

Robert and Eve regress

The Smiths tried different versions of the regression model and held heated discussions about who had produced the better forecasts. They both used ordinary least-squares regression analysis to find the most accurate estimate, but Robert preferred linear regression and Eve insisted on nonlinear.

Robert felt that the use of nonlinear analysis would confuse the councilmembers and the city manager. "Gee, Eve, what are we going to do when they ask questions about squaring and so forth?"

"If the curve fits, use it!" she responded.

Robert agreed with Eve about the need for a good fit but was apprehensive about trying to explain their approach to the council. To forecast taxable sales, the Smiths finally agreed to use the equation described and discussed in the accompanying sidebar, along with projections of the state's personal income obtained from various sources. Their plan was to substitute the state's forecast personal income for Y in the equation and solve for T (taxable transactions), then to multiply taxable transactions by 0.01 (the city's share of taxable sales transactions) to get forecast sales-tax revenue.

Eager to report on their progress, the Smiths presented Manager O'Reilly with their results. They explained that the equation they had selected was the most accurate of the many different specifications they had tried. "We used the mean absolute percentage error (MAPE) to measure accuracy. The regression equation we selected, with a MAPE of 12.2, had the lowest mean (or average) absolute percentage error of the more than fifty equations we estimated."[2]

"What does all this mean to Timber City?" asked O'Reilly.

"Well," said Eve, "the equation indicates that the state's personal income is the most important determinant of your sales-tax revenue. When the state's economy is booming, the way it did during the last decade, your sales-tax revenues grow; when the state is under a recession, as it is now, your sales-tax revenues will decrease."

Surprised, the manager replied, "I didn't realize the problems in the rest of the state affected us that much!"

The forecasting equation

The Smiths selected the following equation to forecast taxable sales:

$$T^2 = 768,000,000,0000 + 13,897.62\ Y^2$$
$$(56.98)$$

where T = Timber City's total taxable transactions, and
Y = the state's personal income in millions.

Because the relationship between T and Y is nonlinear, both T and Y are squared in the equation. The number in parentheses is the "t" value of the coefficient: a "t" greater than 2 indicates that the slope of the trend line differs from a horizontal line (randomness) at a significance level of 0.05 or less.

This equation produced an R^2 of 0.99 and a Durbin-Watson (DW) of 1.42. The R^2 is the percentage of variance in taxable retail sales explained by the independent variable, personal income.

A high R^2 such as this one indicates that personal income is an important determinant of taxable sales. The DW, an important test of serial correlation, suggests that the possibility of serial correlation is not determinable. Thus, the Smiths did not know whether there was systematic under- or overestimation in this equation: a different DW value might have given them the opportunity to draw conclusions on systematic under- or overestimation.

Because the objective is to produce a forecast that is neither over- nor underestimated, determining whether under- or overestimation may have occurred is important not only in the context of regression analysis but also for policy formation. Underestimation suggests that sales-tax revenues actually may be higher than the forecast indicates; overestimation suggests that the forecast may be higher than actual revenues.

The snack tax and the shopping center

According to the state's commission on state finance, the snack tax had increased the state's sales-tax base by 1.5 percent in its first year and would increase the base by 3.3 percent this year and next year. To include this change in their estimates, Robert and Eve increased the estimated tax base that they calculated with the regression equation and personal income.

The Smiths turned to Manager O'Reilly for sales-tax data on the shopping center. "Sales-tax revenue paid by an individual business is confidential; sorry, but I can't give you that type of data," said O'Reilly.

"Well, we don't need the data for each business," responded Robert. "Can you give us all the sales-tax revenue paid by businesses on Fir Avenue?" he asked, remembering that there were few businesses other than the shopping center on Fir.

"I probably could do that," said O'Reilly. "But as consultants to the city, you are obligated to use any data that I can give you for analysis only. You must maintain confidentiality. I'll get you a copy tomorrow if our attorney approves."

"We'll certainly maintain confidentiality," Robert replied.

After examining the sales-tax revenue from Fir Avenue, Robert and Eve estimated gross sales per square foot and concluded that this figure was much lower than the average sales per square foot in the references they had checked.

"Since we don't have any other information, we'll just have to assume that next year's revenues will be the same as this year's revenues," Robert concluded.

"But that's no good; your approach doesn't tie into any behavior that's relevant to policy, or to understanding revenue behavior, or to the economy!" Eve responded.

Robert replied that despite its drawbacks, a forecast based on the assumption that the sales-tax revenues would remain the same still could prove useful for comparisons and for testing against the other forecasts to be made in the study.

Projected revenues

Using the equation they had selected, the forecasts they had obtained for state personal income, and the estimated impacts of the snack tax and the shopping center, the Smiths came up with the predicted sales-tax revenues displayed in Table 2. The lower and upper limits for taxable transactions were calculated using the regression equation and either actual or estimated figures for state personal income. Taxable transactions were multiplied by 0.01 to obtain sales-tax revenues. Revenue from the shopping center was assumed to be the same in this year and for each of the next two years as it was in the previous year. To account for the snack tax enacted in the previous year, the base was expanded by 1.50 percent for that year and 3.30 percent in subsequent years. (Because the snack tax was repealed while the Smiths were in the course of doing their forecast, they later had to reduce their estimate to reflect that change.)

The tax revenue was adjusted upward by 12.7 percent to include accounts receivable and pooled taxable transactions at the state and county levels. To estimate taxable transactions for this year and for each of the next two years, the Smiths used two forecasts of personal income with the regression equation. The state university's forecast of personal income produced a lower range of forecast sales-tax revenues in the "out years" because it was based on a lower projected personal income in the state in those years. The forecasts made by the state commission on finance predicted a higher range of revenues because they were based on a higher forecast level of state personal income.

As soon as they had finished Table 2, the Smiths called on O'Reilly to report their results. Manager O'Reilly examined the table carefully before asking, "What's this 'upper' and 'lower' business? I need a single number for a sales-tax estimate when I make out my budget for next year."

"We can give you a single number if you have to have one, but we think it's better to use a lower and upper bound," replied Robert. "No one can tell you the exact number of dollars that you will collect next year. But we *can* tell you that there's a 95 percent chance that your revenues will fall between the lower and upper limits you see in this table."

"If you want to be sure you have enough sales-tax revenue to cover your expenditures without depleting your reserves, you can use the lower limit of our forecast," Eve added.

"If I do that, I'll have to lay off half a dozen employees," O'Reilly responded. "If the actual revenues come in much higher, *I'll* get the next pink slip! You need to understand that in a small city like this one, reduction in personnel is a reduction in services. The council would have to decide which services to reduce. The politics

Table 2   Estimated sales tax revenues for Timber City with the snack tax and the shopping center (lower and upper ranges representing the 95% limits in the forecast)

Year*	Based on state university's forecast of personal income		Based on state finance commission's forecasts of personal income	
	Lower	Upper	Lower	Upper
CY − 3	$ 749,664	$ 787,616	$ 749,664	$ 787,616
CY − 2	851,198	890,382	851,198	890,382
CY − 1	941,431	980,725	941,431	1,025,253
CY	968,145	1,008,436	984,565	1,025,253
CY + 1	969,363	1,009,035	1,014,261	1,055,070
CY + 2	1,016,098	1,056,955	1,075,264	1,117,694

Note: These forecasts were derived from the consultants' regression results and from forecasts of personal income from the state university and from the state commission on finance for the years indicated in the table.

*"CY" = current year (plus or minus additional years).

of that decision—together with having to deal with the city employees' collective bargaining unit—make this a very sensitive issue.''

''If your only concern is accuracy, you may have overlooked one of the most important advantages of forecasting,'' responded Eve.

''What can be more important than accuracy?'' asked O'Reilly.

''Understanding how different events influence your sales-tax revenue!'' Eve responded. ''Forecasting techniques make it possible to play a game of 'what if.' ''[3]

''For example, what if the economy turns around?'' asked Eve. ''We can give you the spreadsheet that we used to create this table. Then, you can use updated forecasts from the state or from the university to revise our forecasts.''

''So, I can sit here at my computer and take your spreadsheets and develop my own forecast as I get additional information on personal income from the state?'' asked O'Reilly, looking somewhat more satisfied with the table.

''Exactly!'' said Eve.

A visit to the mill

With the sales-tax forecasts behind them, Robert and Eve next began the task of estimating the impact of the mill closing. As a start, they faxed a memo to O'Reilly outlining their analytical methods and explaining the purpose of input-output analysis. A copy of the memo is shown in Exhibit 1, page 37.

After making sure that Manager O'Reilly understood their approach, the Smiths began gathering data on the mill. They met with the mill manager to get data on the number of full-time-equivalent employees and on the locations of their residences. They also asked about the dollar value of the mill's output. Fortunately, the mill manager was very cooperative, and a couple of weeks later the Smiths were able to fax a copy of their preliminary results to Manager O'Reilly. A copy of the fax is shown in Exhibit 2, page 37.

The decision problem

The fax has arrived just as Manager O'Reilly sits down to work over the information he has obtained about the future. He has two different forecasts from Robert and Eve, as well as his own forecast of future city sales-tax revenues. In addition to the disturbing economic indicators and discouraging revenue forecasts, Manager O'Reilly has another problem: some of the councilmembers who own businesses have been saying lately that the future did not look too bad. O'Reilly wonders how receptive the council would be to recommendations that expenditures be reduced.

A further complication is that O'Reilly has his own financial goal: he wants to make sure that he has 10 percent of his general fund revenues set aside, in case a revenue shortfall or some other event brings about unanticipated costs for the city in the coming year. On top of the other troubling possibilities are the mill closure and the possible repeal of the snack tax. According to the Smiths' estimate, the closing would mean a loss of $20,000 in city sales-tax revenues, and the repeal of the snack tax could reduce city sales-tax revenues by 3.3 percent annually.

The continuing bad news about the state's economy, the likelihood of the mill closure, and the protests against the snack tax incline O'Reilly to recommend a conservative budget, but such a recommendation carries a number of risks. First, O'Reilly would be going against the ''gut feelings'' of some councilmembers. Second, an increase in fees or some sort of tax would be likely to anger the public—as would layoffs and a reduction in services.

O'Reilly outlines the critical elements that he has to take into consideration:

1. If the state's economy gets worse, the Smiths' forecasts will have to be revised downward.
2. According to Robert and Eve, the mill closing will reduce sales-tax revenues by about $20,000.

3. If the snack tax is repealed, Timber City's sales-tax revenues will drop by almost $30,000.
4. Last year, the new shopping center more than offset the loss of sales-tax revenues caused by the recession, but this year's sales are lower than expected, and some stores are closing.
5. The recession, the mill closing, the possible repeal of the snack tax, and the slowing sales at the shopping center could combine to push the local economy into a more rapid and more serious downward spiral. The longer the city waits to make cuts, the more severe the cuts may have to be.
6. Timber City needs to keep its existing staff in place just to maintain the low level of public services that its citizens are willing to fund.
7. With so much economic uncertainty, it seems imperative to maintain prudent reserves.

When the council meets tonight to discuss a mid-year budget adjustment, O'Reilly must somehow weave all these factors into his recommendations. What recommendations should he make to the council tonight, both for the balance of the current year and for the forthcoming year?

Discussion questions

1. Evaluate the work of the consultants from the manager's point of view. What new insights and advantages does it provide to the manager? What are some of the problems with the report from the manager's point of view? What, if any, additional information should the manager seek from the consultants?
2. How should the manager deal with the range estimate—as opposed to a point estimate—for the sales-tax projections?
3. Should the new statistical evaluation replace the manager's traditional method of revenue projection?
4. What strategy should the manager develop for approaching the council? How should the manager deal with the council's inclination to view the future as "not too bad"? What might be the impact on the council of a pessimistic economic report and suggestions for layoffs, tax increases, reductions in services, etc.? What might be the impact on the public?
5. Given the community's short-term economic prospects, is the manager overestimating the importance of retaining a general fund reserve?
6. In O'Reilly's place, what would you recommend to the council?

1 IMPLAN is a database and input-output model created by the U.S. Forest Service and the U.S. Office of Emergency Services, both of the U.S. Department of Agriculture; and by the department of agriculture and applied economics at the University of Minnesota.

2 MAPE is the difference between (a) the estimate of Timber City's total taxable transactions from the regression equation for a given year and (b) the actual amount of total transactions that occurred in that year. The error is calculated for each year, and its absolute value is divided by actual taxable transactions for that year. The result is the estimated error, as a percentage of the actual or observed values for each year.

3 See "Time Series and Forecasting," in William F. Matlack, *Statistics for Public Managers* (Itasca, Ill: F.E. Peacock, 1993): "One characteristic of forecasts is that they are nearly always wrong. . . . There is nearly always some error, which is the difference between the actual outcome and the forecasted outcome. . . . Forecasters often make not just a single most likely forecast, but a whole range, running from the most optimistic to the most pessimistic forecasts."

Exhibit 1

To: Neil O'Reilly
        Manager, Timber City

From: Robert and Eve Smith
        Consultants

Re: Overview of input-output analysis

Changes in spending—such as those generated by a mill's closing or by a firm's expansion—can be analyzed using IMPLAN, an input-output model developed by the U.S. Department of Agriculture, the U.S. Forest Service, the U.S. Office of Emergency Services, and the department of agriculture and applied economics at the University of Minnesota. Input-output models provide the only method of analysis that can be used to determine the effect of a change in one industry on all other industries. Given an initial (or primary) change in production in one industry, input-output models thus can be used to determine the *ultimate* change in production, income, and jobs within a county.

The results of a change in production estimated with IMPLAN can be divided into primary, secondary, and tertiary changes. Primary changes are the initial changes in spending for such items as logs and labor. For example, when a mill lays off loggers, the reduction in the mill's expenditures on wages is a primary change in spending. This primary spending change will decrease production and destroy jobs, and the resulting secondary and tertiary changes will cause the ultimate impact to be much larger than the initial change. In other words, the initial change will have a multiplier effect on the economy.

Secondary impacts are caused by the primary changes in spending. They result when the loggers affected by primary cuts in production purchase from other firms fewer inputs, such as gasoline and truck repair services. Like the primary changes, these secondary changes also cause production to decline and jobs to be cut—but in industries besides the one in which the primary changes occurred. For example, if fewer loggers are bringing their trucks in for repair, the repair shop may lay off a mechanic.

Tertiary changes result when people spend less because of the primary and secondary impacts on their incomes. For example, loggers who are laid off by the mill may not be able to afford medical care; mechanics who lose their jobs because fewer loggers are bringing in trucks for repair also may spend less on medical care. The reduction in medical expenditures is a tertiary change that will result in fewer jobs in clinics and hospitals. Thus, tertiary changes as well as secondary changes contribute to the multiplier effect.

Exhibit 2

To: Neil O'Reilly
        Manager, Timber City

From: Robert and Eve Smith
        Consultants

Re: Impact of mill closing on jobs, income, and output in Bunyan County

We used IMPLAN to forecast the impact on Bunyan County if the mill closes. The initial loss will be 328 jobs at the mill, but once multiplier effects are taken into account, the loss will be more than 1,200 jobs and almost $64 million in income, as shown in Table A. The slightly lower losses under the heading "With unemployment benefits" are based on the assumption that the laid-off workers will receive an average of $210 per week in unemployment compensation for twelve months.

Table A Changes in jobs, income, and output in Bunyan County due to the mill closure (current-year dollars)

	Without unemployment benefits	With unemployment benefits
Change in jobs	1,231	1,188
Change in income	$63.9 million	$61.9 million
Change in output	$95.5 million	$192.1 million

Note: These estimates were developed using IMPLAN, an input-output model developed by the U.S. Department of Agriculture, the U.S. Forest Service, the U.S. Office of Emergency Services, and the department of agriculture and applied economics at the University of Minnesota.

When the mill stops buying logs, there will be approximately 197 jobs lost in logging, which, after the mill itself, will be the second-hardest-hit industry in the county. Other hard-hit industries will be retail and wholesale trade, in which a total of almost 190 jobs will be lost because laid-off workers will spend less. Approximately 55 jobs will be lost in restaurants and bars, which are particularly sensitive to the decreases in income that result from job losses. And about 31 jobs will be lost in hospitals because (1) some laid-off workers will seek employment outside the county, and (2) the unemployed workers who remain in the county will not have medical insurance.

Table B shows the forecast for the impact of the mill closing on Timber City's sales-tax revenues for this year and the two years after this. The IMPLAN analysis indicates that if the mill were to close on December 31 of this year, there would be a decrease in county income of approximately $61.9 million during the period when laid-off workers could get unemployment benefits; once the workers ceased collecting unemployment, the loss would be $63.9—some $2 million greater.

To estimate the impact of the countywide income loss on Timber City's taxable transactions, we regressed Timber City's taxable transactions on state personal income. We estimate the loss in Timber City's sales-tax revenues to be between $18,000 and $20,000 each year. In the second year after the closure, the loss of sales-tax revenue will be about $18,500 to $20,500. Part of this increase is due to the fact that some laid-off workers will not have had a chance to get new jobs and will no longer be eligible for unemployment insurance benefits.

Table B Impact of 328-worker mill's closure on Timber city's sales-tax revenues

Year*	Without closure		With closure	
	Lower	Upper	Lower	Upper
CY	$ 968,145	$1,025,253	na	na
CY + 1	969,363	1,055,070	$949,539	$1,036,557
CY + 2	1,016,098	1,117,694	995,655	1,098,602

Note: The estimated loss in income due to the closure of a 328-worker mill was forecast with IMPLAN. This change in income was multiplied by the marginal change in taxable transactions per dollar of income derived from our regression of Timber City's taxable transactions with Bunyan County's personal income. We assumed that the mill would close on the last day of the current year and that the 152 Timber City residents who are mill employees would remain in Timber city collecting unemployment benefits until the last day of the next year.
*"CY" = current year (plus additional years).

4 Preparing the budget

Editor's introduction

Teachers of budgeting and finance love to remark that all public policy is ultimately made during the budget process. No matter what policy the legislative body might adopt, the actual policy is fashioned during its implementation, and the implementation of every policy is shaped by money—by the amount of money available and by the constraints put on its use. The money decisions, in turn, are made during the budget process.

Two separate budgetary activities form the heart of the budget process. The first is planning and development—the policymaking that goes into the preparation of the budget. The second is budget implementation; it involves the policy decisions needed to adjust ongoing policies to the new realities that emerge during the course of a budget year. Both of these processes, but especially the planning and development phase, are described in this case, "Welcome to the New Town Manager?" The second activity, budget implementation, is depicted more fully in the next case, "County Prison Overtime."

As "Welcome to the New Town Manager?" portrays so well, budget planning and preparation in local government is policymaking. It is the point at which the policy makers, including the manager and finance officer, must revisit existing policies in service priorities, service levels, tax policy, service charges, capital improvements, and debt management. Each such policy must be examined in terms of present and projected future circumstances, and then all must be reconciled into a single package, or budget. Linked together in that budget, they constitute an operating strategy for the accomplishment of community objectives in a manner consistent with the community's long-term values and short-term political preferences. As Manager Holbrook found in Opportunity, the task is as daunting as it sounds.

Each of the policy choices that must be made in the case has an apparently obvious answer, but each such answer requires a fundamental change from past policy—and each such change would encounter political obstacles. A community grown accustomed to pay-as-you-go capital improvement financing, subsidized water and sewer service, stable tax rates, and established service levels maintained by deficit financing will not easily or willingly accept wholesale changes in such financial policies. Yet all must be reevaluated; business as usual is no longer an option in Opportunity.

"Welcome to the New Town Manager?" also describes every manager's worst nightmare: an apparently healthy and tranquil government suddenly thrown into crisis conditions with a plethora of hard choices to be made and little time to make them. To make matters worse, the crises all emerge during Manager Holbrook's first two weeks on the job. She must begin acting on them without even the opportunity to establish her reputation or build her management team.

The challenge confronting Manager Holbrook may sound more fictional than real. Unfortunately, truth is often stranger than fiction, and the situation in this case has been all too real for all too many managers. Hard budget choices are more the rule than the exception in today's local government, and unexpected problems all too often confront new managers early in their tenure.

Such daunting challenges are the "stuff" of local government management; they are the "stuff" with which managers must cope; they are the "stuff" from which managers derive the satisfaction of building better communities.

Case 4
Welcome to the new town manager?
Mary Jane Kuffner Hirt

Background

Opportunity is a suburban community of 9,200 people located six miles from a declining industrial/corporate center in the mid-Atlantic region. The eight-square-mile municipality, composed of a series of hills and valleys and shaped like a horseshoe, wraps around one of the most affluent communities in the United States. While the municipality is primarily single-family residential in nature, its treasure is a 600-acre regional research and industrial park. The site is home to more than 125 enterprises that employ about 8,000 people and concentrate on light manufacturing, research and development, and wholesale food, beverage, and pharmaceutical distribution. The mostly white-collar community has a low poverty level (1.6 percent), an average elderly population (11.7 percent), and above-average socio-economic characteristics. Population growth is minimal because of a growing number of empty-nesters and smaller-sized families.

The politics

A home rule community since 1976, Opportunity has a council-manager form of government. Its seven-member council consists of a president and vice president elected at large and five other members elected by district. The five district representatives, elected last November, include three new members and two incumbents. The president and vice president are in the middle of their terms.

The new council, which has a 4-to-3 Republican/Democrat split, includes three attorneys, an educator, an engineer/local business operator, a self-employed businessman, and a retiree. The council tends to operate as a group and generally does not split on decisions along political party lines. Most councilmembers adhere to the philosophy that the day-to-day operations belong under the direction of the manager; council's role is to concentrate on policy and decision responsibilities.

The community has thirty-four full-time and five part-time employees. Services provided by employees include police protection, public works (road, storm, sanitary sewer, and water system services), recreation, zoning, planning and development, and general administration. The town provides financial support to three volunteer fire departments, an ambulance service, and a multijurisdictional library and community center.

In January, the town manager unexpectedly resigned. The council then spent four months searching for a new manager, ending up with two semifinalist candidates from a field of ninety: the current assistant manager and the manager from a nearby community. In a vote of 4 to 2 with one abstention, the council selected the manager from the nearby community.

Town finances

The municipality has strong, stable financial characteristics. The operating and capital budgets for the current year total approximately $3.3 million (Tables 1 and 2).

Table 1 Current year budget

Revenue		
Real estate tax	$ 894,640	27.0%
Earned-income tax	959,000	29.0
Other taxes	105,000	3.0
Licenses, fees, permits	72,490	2.2
Sewer fees	369,000	11.0
Water fees	116,700	3.5
Intergovernmental grants	177,575	5.4
Interest earnings	62,000	2.0
Charges for service	45,750	1.4
Miscellaneous	19,000	0.5
Use of fund balance	491,390	15.0
Total	$3,312,545	100.0%
Expenditures		
General government	$ 377,181	12.0%
Public safety	758,012	23.0
Engineering/code enforcement	154,870	5.0
Sanitation	176,771	5.0
Public works	541,750	16.0
Water service	158,090	6.0
Sewer service	330,800	9.0
Parks/recreation	108,180	3.0
Debt service	168,261	5.0
Capital program	538,630	16.0
Total	$3,312,545	100.0%

Table 2 Current year capital program

Road improvements	$253,000 + $77,400 (general revenue sharing)
Sanitary sewer	113,000
Water system	46,280
Municipal buildings	32,350
Public works equipment and vehicles	54,000
Comprehensive plan	10,000
Fire department subsidy	30,000
Total	$538,630

The last tax increase occurred seven years ago, when one mill was added to the property tax. The revenue base primarily is composed of two local taxes: real estate and earned-income taxes (see Table 1). Prior councils created a tax structure that balanced the taxpaying responsibility between residents and the businesses located in the regional industrial park. Consequently, the property tax, at 10.75 mills, is a little over half of the general-purpose maximum rate of 20.00 mills and with a 97 percent collection rate generates about 27.0 percent, or $894,640, of total revenues.

In addition, the community has taken advantage of its unlimited authority to set tax rates under home rule and levies a 0.9 percent earned-income tax, which yields $959,000 (see Table 1). (One-tenth percent of earned-income tax produces approximately $106,500.) Water and sewer utility fees provide another 14.5 percent, and grants from the state for highway maintenance, police pensions, and volunteer fire relief funds, plus federal revenue sharing, make up about 5.4 percent of total revenues. Additional tax revenues come from real estate transfer and occupation privilege taxes.

The community is recognized as one with high service levels, and residents have not indicated any dissatisfaction with present taxing levels. Of note on the expenditure side of the current year's budget, as shown in Table 1, are the low annual debt-service payment of $168,261 and the planned capital outlay of $538,630, representing 5.0 percent and 16.0 percent of the total budget, respectively. By tradition, the town council tends to follow a practice of "pay-as-you-go" financing for capital improvements.

Ongoing councilmanic debate about annual expenditures has related to the water and sanitary sewer systems' lack of financial self-sufficiency. Revenues provided via sewer and water service fees have covered the town's annual expense for the sewage treatment services provided by a regional sanitary authority, other sewer-related operating costs, and part of the expense of purchasing water from three outside sources for resale to municipal customers. Increases of 37.5 percent in water and 20 percent in sewer rates to raise an additional $90,000 were factored into the revenue estimates for the current year.

Sewer fees for the year have been estimated to generate $369,000 from about 3,000 residential and commercial customers, even though sewer system operating expenses have been estimated at $330,800 and capital expenses at $113,000. Approximately 700 water customers this year are expected to pay about $116,700 to partially offset water operating costs estimated at $158,090 and capital projects of some $46,280. However, as of May 31, the council had taken no action to implement the rate changes.

Other short-term budgetary concerns include:

1. Finding money to finance major improvements to the "aging and deteriorating" sewer and water systems and municipal building
2. Coping with the impending loss of $75,000 in intergovernmental funds previously used to finance a portion of the annual road improvement program
3. Identifying new sources of revenue to make up for using accumulated surpluses of approximately $880,000 to balance the annual budget over the preceding four-year period.

Under the home rule charter, the town manager is charged with responsibility for proposing, implementing, and monitoring the budget adopted by the council. In practice, the operating and capital funds budget has been used as the community's principal tool for establishing short- and long-term service and project priorities. An independent financial audit is performed annually.

The case

The spring in Opportunity was a time of memory-making significance for the community as a whole and for many council and municipal staff members in particular. By mid-May, the council finally had completed its comprehensive and somewhat contentious search for a new town manager and selected Jennifer Holbrook. With her arrival, municipal operations could resume a regular course of activity. The attention of the council and staff could be refocused on an ambitious agenda of community planning; on the consideration of a newly proposed, mixed-use riverfront zoning district; on the development of a systematic road improvement process; and on the implementation of the annual capital program.

However, within just two weeks—the week before the manager's arrival and her first week on the job—two unanticipated and unrelated disasters occurred that redirected the interests and efforts of the community, council, and staff for the remaining seven months of the year.

The initial disaster was financial. Four months into the fiscal year, the independent audit report for the prior year revealed a closing fund balance of $275,122, approximately $469,000 less than anticipated. During budget preparation, a surplus of $744,456 had been projected, and the council had allocated $491,390 of it to balance the town's current-year budget. The smaller fund balance resulted from a major miscalculation: the month of September's expenditures had not been included in the year-end estimate of total expenses. Consequently, the municipality was looking at a potential year-end deficit of at least $210,000. Manager Holbrook was informed of the situation by the assistant manager in a memo dated May 16. Because the town council had not yet been advised of this financial crisis, it became the manager's responsibility to inform the council at her first workshop meeting on May 27.

The second catastrophe was natural. On May 30, a flash flood fueled by one-and-one-half inches of rainfall in a little less than one hour devastated an eight-community area. A typically harmless stream became a raging deathtrap for a neighborhood of thirty-eight families, killing eight people and causing millions of dollars of public and private property damage. The initial cost to the town for cleanup operations and repairs to the heavily traveled Brownshill Bridge was about $96,000. Principal among the private problems that later posed significant public responsibilities were the contamination of residential water wells by on-lot septic systems destroyed during the flood, and citizen demands for stream-related flood prevention and protection measures.

A third event, less dramatic but potentially important for the community over the long term, concerned the manner in which planning and evaluation for the annual road improvement program had been conducted. At the council's workshop on May 27, councilmembers had directed Manager Holbrook to develop a comprehensive and systematic process for identifying and funding road improvements. If such a system were not proposed by November 15 and adopted by the council by December 31 of the current year, allocations for subsequent years' road improvements would be reduced by about two-thirds, to $100,000. This ultimatum had resulted from the council's growing frustration over the previous three years, during which three staff engineers had proposed three different road improvement processes for the town.

The decision problem

Now, in the first week of June, Jennifer Holbrook faces an urgent need to develop an effective operating strategy for the next seven months. Given the circumstances, she has to address simultaneously both long- and short-term problems and issues.

The current financial crisis

To minimize the current financial crisis, quick action has to be taken. At mid-year, given the council's failure to authorize the proposed sewer and water fee increases, only significant cuts in operating expenses, capital expenditures, or both will balance the budget. Within the general fund, major reductions can be achieved by deferring the replacement of a police officer and the addition of a new technician in the community development area. Additional general fund savings, though lesser ones, can be accomplished if discretionary expenses within each program area are minimized by department heads for the rest of the year.

Hiring a police officer is more urgent than adding a technician. The police department generally operates with a staff of twelve: nine patrol officers and a sergeant, lieutenant, and superintendent. Forty-seven miles of road stretching across eight square miles requires that two officers be on duty each shift to provide timely response. At this time, the force is down to ten members, with the resignation of one officer and the loss of another for a long time with a back injury. To maintain all shifts with at least two officers has required a consistent use of overtime in the first half of the year. With summer vacations further reducing available personnel, overtime costs certainly would exceed budgetary expectations. The civil service commission has conducted the screening process for a replacement police officer and recently has posted an eligibility list. The council, civil service commissioners, and local citizens are anxious to see the vacancy filled. To delay hiring a replacement would be difficult, but potential savings by not paying a full-time salary with benefits could be $30,000.

No action has been taken thus far regarding the technician. The position has been requested principally to provide in-house assistance for the town's full-time engineer. The new employee would help prepare plans and perform inspections for water, sewer, and road construction projects. In the past, these services had been procured on an as-needed basis from local engineering firms or independent contractors. With a greater number of capital projects scheduled for the next several years, the staff strongly recommends the addition of a full-time employee. Even though $25,000 had been budgeted for the technician's position, in March the council had tabled action to initiate the hiring process when it requested a more detailed job description.

Holbrook recognizes that discretionary spending across all programs for materials and supplies and minor equipment might be reduced by 5 to 10 percent and could provide $11,000 to $22,000 in general operating savings. To achieve this aim, she could direct all department supervisors to review such purchases carefully for the remainder of the year. Given an assessment of prior years' actual spending versus budget allocations, this request likely would not affect service levels.

The major remaining capital projects for the year include the road improvement program ($330,400), sanitary sewer reconstruction in the regional industrial park to replace pumping stations with gravity lines ($113,000), municipal building improvements ($32,350), water system rehab ($46,280), and purchase of public works trucks and vehicle testing equipment ($54,000). Only one of the projects, sewer reconstruction in the industrial park, is an absolute necessity. County health and state environmental officials have mandated corrective action because twice per day, Monday through Friday, the pumping stations cannot keep up with demand. Raw sewage is being discharged directly into a local stream. Construction of gravity lines over a two-year period would eliminate this problem.

Future financial concerns

The present situation is further complicated by the need to address other budget-related concerns in preparation for the next fiscal year. According to the home rule charter, budget preparation must start officially in July, with the development of a five-year capital plan. The next year's proposed operating and capital budgets must be presented to the council by November 1.

Three major issues face Manager Holbrook as she deals with the current crisis and starts planning for the next budget year. The first issue involves financial policy governing utility operations: should general fund revenues continue to subsidize the community's water and sanitary sewer systems? Earlier in the year, council's reluctance to act decisively to raise sewer and water fees had reflected the complicated nature of the situation. The recommended sewer rate increase of 20 percent would add $60,000, and total revenue generated for sewer services would be $369,000. With the rate increase, revenues would have covered annual operating expenses of about $330,000 and left $39,000 for capital expenses. The $39,000 partially would have offset the initial phase of the $226,000 sewer reconstruction project for the industrial park ($113,000 was in the capital budget for the year). A 37.5 percent water rate increase would have added $30,000 in water revenues, to produce a total of $116,700 for the year. Essentially, this amount would cover two-thirds of the $158,090 annual operating costs, though none of this year's $46,280 capital expense.

Basically, the council has been wrestling with whether it can justify rate increases to make the utilities more self-sufficient at the same time as it recognizes that previous municipal inaction has created part of the problem. The community has not maintained the water distribution system properly. The leaking system probably has lost 20 to 25 percent of the water purchased by the town for distribution before it reaches customer meters. Rust and sediment in the water provided to about 150 customers routinely ruin laundries and, in many cases, force residents to buy bottled water for drinking purposes.

The council also hesitates to penalize customers by increasing sewer rates to correct the problems of the poorly designed sanitary sewer system in the twenty-year-old regional industrial park.

To add further difficulty to this dilemma, each year delinquent water and sewer fees have been in the range of 20 to 25 percent. The auditor's estimate of the accumulated value of uncollected fees at the end of the prior year is about $250,000. Implementation of an effective collection process for delinquent water and sewer fees has been hampered by inconsistencies among computerized payment records and by the absence of an authorized policy to end water services for chronic delinquents.

Dealing with this issue would require balancing fiscal demands with the identification of appropriate community-wide and customer responsibilities. The solution to achieving self-sufficiency or near-sufficiency for either or both services undoubtedly would require rate adjustments, as well as adoption of a tough stance on delinquencies. It likely would cause a stir within the community.

The second major issue that Holbrook faces deals with the budget balance: over $880,000 in surplus funds has been used to balance the municipality's budget in the last four years. The fund balance is now depleted. How should future budgets be balanced? Should services be cut, tax rates increased, new fees for service established, or some combination of options be developed to finance the $200,000 to $300,000 annual shortfall caused by the repeated reliance on the fund balance? (A garbage fee of $60 per year based on 3,000 households to fund the $180,000 garbage collection and disposal contract has been rejected as a new revenue source for the current fiscal year.)

The third issue concerns financing infrastructure improvements in the community: should the council abandon the previously established policy to fund capital projects on a pay-as-you-go basis? Is it time to look at various debt financing options to address the community's major road, sewer, water, and municipal building projects? The comprehensive road improvement program developed in response to the council's mandate indicates that $5 million to $6 million should be spent over the next ten years to upgrade the town's forty-seven miles of roads. In addition, reconstruction of major segments of the water distribution system is estimated to cost $750,000, and about $250,000 in municipal building improvements is required, some of which are needed to comply with handicapped-accessibility requirements.

Debt-service expense for the current year is just over $168,000, 5.0 percent of the total budget. Outstanding principal and interest on existing short- and long-term debt is $525,500 and will be repaid fully within the next five years. For the flood-affected areas, where damaged on-lot septic systems have contaminated about nine out of ten of the residential water wells, special grants or loans might be available to fund a part of the construction of public water and sanitary sewer systems. Estimated costs for the water and sewer systems are $326,700 and $1.1 million, respectively.

The urgency of the circumstances outlined above preclude Manager Holbrook from assessing with care her new staff's capacity or from building a management team. Instead, she essentially has to rely on staff and department heads to provide the necessary assistance and cooperation. Taking time to discuss and establish guidelines to facilitate daily council-manager interaction at workshops and public meetings also is not feasible. As a result, the development of a sound strategy to address the remaining seven months of the year poses a challenge of major proportions for the manager, the existing staff, and the council.

In formulating her plans, furthermore, the manager has to assess the political consequences of various actions. The council has not been willing in the past to make hard decisions on tax and fee increases to keep the budget balanced. Without any chance to test the political climate further, she must decide whether to take bold political initiatives, calling for major changes in town fiscal policy, using the recent crises as justification for recommendations that might cost her needed support on the council. Should she play it safe politically and search for answers that will patch the town through the immediate crisis while forgoing needed improvements? Or should she find some accommodation between these two courses of action? As a newcomer, she does not know how much support she can expect from the council during her first weeks on the job, how the community will respond to tough new measures, or even how much blame for the current situation can be passed off onto the former manager and former councils. What she does know is that the council has not been willing to face up to tough choices on town finances.

Holbrook is, in short, not yet settled in the community; she has had no time to build a base of support; and now she faces the need to make immediate decisions that could threaten her future effectiveness as a leader.

Clearly, she has two decisions to make. First, she has to decide how much personal political risk she is willing to take. Then, and most important, she has to devise two sets of financial recommendations: (1) she must propose adjustments in the current budget to keep from overspending the community's reserves; and (2) she must suggest policies that will restore balance to next year's budget. And she has to make these budget recommendations even while responding to the aftermath of the floods. Decisions—lots of decisions—have to be made fast.

Discussion questions

1. What adjustments should the manager recommend to the council to alleviate Opportunity's projected budget deficit for the current year? (Hint: Revise Tables 1 and 2 in the text.) Should local residents be advised of the financial crisis? If so, what should be communicated, when, how, and by whom?

2. What budget strategy should the manager recommend to the council for the next fiscal year to achieve a balanced budget? Remember that next year's budget must: (a) maintain the community's high level of services; (b) respond to the pressures for infrastructure repairs and improvements created by the flood; and (c) address the need for major water, sewer, and road improvements. What combination of changes, if any, in tax and revenue policies, expenditure policies, capital budget policies, and capital expenditure financing policies is most likely to produce a balanced budget consistent with the council's and community's expectations?

3. Traditionally, the first few months on the job for a new manager are critical as relationships with the council, staff, volunteer organizations, and community are forged. Given the circumstances of this situation, the manager's getting-acquainted opportunity has lasted about four days. What operating style should the manager adopt to address the crises faced by Opportunity?

   Are effective managerial styles essentially different for handling crises versus routine operations? If the manager effectively manages these crises, are there any difficulties that might arise to hinder her development of positive, long-term relationships with the council and staff? Explain.

4. Assess the assistant manager's decision to defer any communication of the town's fiscal problem to the council until after the new manager's arrival. What, if any, are the potential implications of this action? How should the manager deal with the assistant manager regarding this matter?

5 Implementing the budget

Editor's introduction

Policymaking in the budget process certainly does not end when the budget is adopted. This is particularly true in local governments that operate under mandates—legal, political, and economic—to keep costs within available revenues. As the budget year unfolds, and as changing economic conditions, unanticipated needs, and other circumstances beyond administrative control make their impact felt on both revenues and expenditures, mid-year corrections in authorized spending levels are frequently necessary. Further, every budget requires that line items be stretched over the year, costs contained, budget policies enforced, and economies in spending encouraged.

Thus is the stage set for continuing dialogue, and sometimes confrontation, between the budget office and line departments. This case, "County Prison Overtime," provides a classic example of the difficulties of budget implementation.

The dispute itself follows a typical pattern. What starts as an exchange of memos between fellow department heads becomes acrimonious. Questions of jurisdiction, expertise, and even motives arise. The dispute soon involves the county administrator, but not before it has come to the attention of the elected chairman of the county board.

As is almost always the case in such management problems, there is no clear right or wrong. And with two valuable and competent subordinates involved, the administrator finds himself searching for a win-win solution, or at least one that will not present an obvious defeat or embarrassment for either party. An overriding consideration is the need for a solution that falls within the constraints posed by budget policy and local politics.

Any solution, furthermore, will have policy implications, both for the budget and for the way in which the county prison system is managed. Policy changes always pose a degree of threat to administrators, especially when they are perceived as caused by other administrators who lack an understanding of the reasons for the current policy.

This case also provides a glimpse into a little-known and less-understood public service function: the management of a county correctional facility. The dispute centers on overtime pay for correctional officers, and the solution must take account of the undeniable need for, and the working conditions of, such officers. In the case of public safety personnel, any budgetary saving must be accomplished without a serious reduction in service or increased danger to the public.

The solution thus requires good analysis of relevant data, faithfulness to operating budgetary policies, sensitivity to the personalities of those involved, and, as always in local government, an eye on the politicians watching from the sidelines. In short, this case poses a typical challenge to the creativity of the public-sector decision maker.

(*Note*: This case was published in slightly different form in ICMA's *Managing Local Government: Cases in Decision Making*. The version printed here has been revised to include more of the kinds of data needed by managers/finance officers to find a solution to the problem posed.)

Case 5
County prison overtime
Tom Mills

Background

Franklin County is a suburban/rural county located in one of the mid-Atlantic states; it adjoins a large eastern city. Franklin County has a land area of 650 square miles; a population of approximately 500,000; and 45 local governments that consist of boroughs, villages, and townships. The local governments have their own police forces but lack secure holding facilities for defendants arrested and bound over by the local magistrates for trial in the county courts.

The county provides all criminal justice system services from the county courthouse located in Franklinville, the county seat. On a tract of county-owned land just outside Franklinville, the county operates two detention facilities: a small, medium-security facility for juveniles and a large, modern, medium-security facility for both male and female adult detainees. The latter facility, called the county prison, has a capacity of approximately 340 inmates and is maintained and operated by a staff of 181 employees.

Franklin County's chief law-making and administrative authority is the elected county commission, which is vested with both executive and legislative powers. Voters also elect a number of administrative officers—including the sheriff, the controller, and the district attorney—and the judges of the county court, called the supreme court of common pleas.

The county commission consists of three members elected countywide for four-year terms. The county code requires that one of the three commissioners be a member of the opposing, or minority, party. The county is predominantly Republican, and members of that party regularly control the countywide elective offices. The county commission, perhaps owing to its higher visibility, has occasionally been controlled by a Democratic majority.

The county commissioners appoint a county administrator, all nonelected department heads, and the members of most county boards and commissions. The day-to-day operation of the county is the responsibility of the county administrator, who is a professional local government manager recruited and appointed on the basis of technical competence. The county boasts a commitment to professionalism. The county administrator recruits and hires his or her own staff and has been responsible for securing the appointments of the finance director, the personnel director, and the director of purchasing.

The county code constrains the county commissioners' powers of appointment in some instances. The power to appoint the director of the department of corrections, who oversees both the county prison and the juvenile rehabilitation center, is vested in a prison board. The prison board is composed of the president judge of the supreme court of common pleas or that judge's designee, the district attorney, the sheriff, the controller, and the three county commissioners. Five of the seven members of the board were Republicans at the time this case began.

The case

In the previous election, the Democratic party had won the majority of seats on the county commission by taking what proved to be the more popular position on a critical environmental issue. In hopes of reelection, the Democratic commissioners instituted a cost containment program that, if successful, would enable them to complete their term without raising taxes. The commissioners issued a directive to all department heads instructing them to implement economies wherever possible.

The county administrator, George Truly, was given the principal responsibility for implementing the cost containment program. He, in turn, had charged the finance director, Donald Dexter, with much of the operating responsibility for the program.

After monitoring the expenditures of the county prison, Dexter was convinced that overtime expenditures were out of control. He had met on several occasions with Charles Goodheart, the director of corrections, and had called him almost weekly in an effort to reduce overtime costs. In Dexter's view, those contacts had been of little value because overtime expenditures continued at what he regarded as an excessive rate. Somewhat reluctantly, he decided to go ''on record.'' He dictated what was to be the first in a series of memorandums.

March 12

TO: Charles R. Goodheart, Director of Corrections

FROM: Donald D. Dexter, Finance Director

SUBJECT: Excessive Prison Overtime

Pursuant to the county commissioners' directive of January 8 establishing the cost containment program, my staff and I have been closely monitoring the overtime expenditures incurred in the operation of the county prison. We have had several meetings and numerous telephone conversations regarding this matter with both you and your key staff members—all to no avail. Overtime expenditures have continued to rise and might well exceed the budget allocation. This I find to be particularly distressing because we had every hope that this was one area of your operation in which we could effect significant savings.

I would greatly appreciate it if you would provide me, at your first opportunity, with a detailed justification for the current rate of overtime usage and your plans to keep such expenditures to an absolute minimum.

cc: George S. Truly, County Administrator
     Frank Friendly, Personnel Director

Before sending this memorandum, Dexter had given the action considerable thought and had concluded that, even if the memorandum was a bit strong, it was warranted in this case.

In the weeks that followed, Dexter continued to scrutinize the prison payroll records but did not observe any reduction in the use of overtime. He was about to schedule yet another meeting with Goodheart when he received the following memorandum.

April 5

TO: Donald D. Dexter, Finance Director

FROM: Charles R. Goodheart, Director of Corrections

SUBJECT: Response to Your Request for Information Regarding Overtime
           Expenditures

You indicated in your memorandum of March 12 that you felt we were utilizing an excessive amount of overtime. I welcome the opportunity to explain what might appear to be excessive overtime usage but which really is no more than prudent prison management.

You will recall that during the budget hearings last year, I shared with you information on overtime usage in the four surrounding counties. Each of these counties has a comparable prison system, and, as I noted then, each uses more overtime than we do.

You must remember that I requested $434,400 as an overtime allocation for the current fiscal year (including holiday overtime). The overtime figure that was allocated to this department was substantially less. When budget allocations were announced, there was no explanation for the reduced overtime figure other than a general statement—which certainly is appropriate for you as finance director to make—that times were difficult, money was tight, and every effort must be made to curtail unnecessary expenditures. Although I accept these comments in the spirit in which they were made, I still am held responsible and accountable to the prison board for operating a safe and secure correctional institution. Prisons are potentially very dangerous, and that danger can be averted only by keeping staffing levels at safe and realistic levels.

As we both know, there are many justifiable causes for overtime usage in a prison setting. In the following paragraphs I'll attempt to identify the major causes.

Turnover   During last year and continuing into this year, we have experienced high levels of turnover among our correctional officers. When staff members leave, we are required to fill their posts, which we do through the use of overtime. The problem continues during recruitment for replacements and during the three-week training course to which all recruits are sent. When you add the two-to-four-week delay in filling positions to the three-week training period, you can readily see that a considerable amount of overtime might be involved. Turnover is perhaps our most critical problem. Previously, I sent you a detailed commentary on our turnover experience. Over the past several years, I have told everyone willing to listen that there is a strong relationship between turnover in a correctional institution and overtime expenditures.

First of all, entry-level correctional officers are poorly paid, and, as I've told the county commissioners at every budget hearing, that is certainly true in our case. Second, this is a very difficult profession, and prison personnel are continually required to work at very high stress levels. Finally, we enjoy very little public esteem, and the working conditions can on occasion be very unpleasant. Small wonder that there is high turnover not only in our prisons but in prisons all across this country. When a staff member leaves, the need to fill the post continues. Unless the prison board tells me that it does not want me to fill vacant posts, I will continue to do so, and I have no choice but to use overtime.

Hospital watches   Whenever an inmate requires inpatient treatment in a local hospital, I must provide the necessary security. Recently, two inmates were hospitalized. For each day of hospitalization, we provided two correctional officers per shift, three shifts per day, for a total of forty-eight hours of coverage. As you can see, the time mounts up rapidly. We have no fat in our shift complements; therefore, when a need like this arises, it must be covered with overtime.

Emergency situations   Whenever there is reason to believe that inmates might be planning an action that could endanger the security of the institution, I adopt an emergency plan that puts all supervisors on twelve-hour shifts. I do not place this institution on an emergency footing for any trivial or illusory cause. Those instances in which I have used emergency overtime have been fully justified, and I stand by my actions.

Sick leave   Our sick leave usage compares favorably with that of other county departments that enjoy less trying working conditions. Still, when a correctional officer calls in sick, his or her position must be filled, and it is usually filled by the use of overtime. We can't call in a replacement on one hour's notice on the person's day off, upset his or her family life, and worsen a bad morale situation simply to cover an eight-hour shift. We feel that the use of overtime in these situations is the most sensible solution.

Workers' compensation I have frequently remarked on this problem in the past. Today, we are filling two posts that are vacant as a result of workers' compensation claims against the county. When an employee is injured on the job and a doctor certifies that he or she may not work, I have no choice but to utilize overtime to fill the post. I simply don't have any slack resources that would permit me to do otherwise.

Reserve duty Under the laws of this state, all staff members who are members of bona fide military reserve units are authorized to take fifteen days of paid military leave annually. When they depart for their military training, their posts remain, and we are responsible for filling them. The problem is exacerbated by the tendency of both military leave and vacations to cluster in the summer months. Another aspect of military reserve duty also generates overtime. Our correctional officers are scheduled around the clock and frequently are scheduled to work on a weekend when they are expected to attend reserve drills. Under the policy adopted by the county commissioners, the reservists may take "no pay" time and fulfill their reserve obligations. While the county saves their straight-time pay, I am forced to use overtime to fill their posts.

Vacations We do make a concerted effort to schedule vacations so as not to result in overtime expenditures. Unfortunately, as a direct result of our lean staffing, on occasion we must resort to overtime to permit our correctional officers to enjoy the vacations they have earned.

Training programs Compared with the standard advocated by national authorities, our training efforts are extremely modest. We provide equal employment opportunity training, particularly with respect to our female correctional officers, and some supervisory training. In addition, we provide training in interpersonal communication skills—training I regard as essential in an institution such as ours. Because our shift schedules contain no fat, personnel must be brought in for training on their days off, which, of course, results in overtime.

The major causes of our overtime expenditure are as noted above. I have brought these problems and their causes to the attention of the county commissioners at every budget hearing over the past nine years. Our staff utilization records and overtime documentation are available to anyone who wishes to review them. We have nothing to hide.

I don't mean to be flippant or discourteous, but frankly I'm no wizard. I cannot operate this institution without a reasonable overtime allocation any more than the Jews of antiquity could make bricks without straw. For you to insist that I do so strikes me as every bit as unreasonable as was the order of the Pharaoh's overseer.

If you can provide specific suggestions regarding policies or methodologies that you feel will assist in overtime reduction without compromising safe and efficient operation of this institution, please be assured that we will be happy to work with you in implementing them. We are open to any thoughtful and constructive recommendations that you or your staff may have. In the meantime, you might consider funding a comprehensive study of our staffing needs, including the need for overtime, by a nationally recognized group specializing in the field of corrections.

cc: Members of the County Prison Board
    George S. Truly, County Administrator
    Frank Friendly, Personnel Director

Dexter read the memorandum twice, his feelings alternating between anger and frustration. He regarded Goodheart highly, knowing him to be a caring individual and a respected corrections professional. "But clearly," thought Dexter, "he's no administrator. I asked him for a detailed justification of his use of overtime and his plans to keep those expenditures to a minimum, and what did he do? He offered me a lesson in biblical history and tried to put the monkey on my back with that bit about 'any thoughtful and constructive recommendations' I might have—baloney!" Dexter noted that Goodheart had twice mentioned his accountability to the county prison board and had been ingracious enough to copy the prison board members on the memorandum. "That," thought Dexter sourly, "is just a brazen example of saber rattling. Maybe he thinks that if he can broaden the controversy by bringing in the prison board, he can get me off his case. Not likely!" Still angry, he spun in his chair, picked up the mike of his recording machine, and dictated his reply.

Meanwhile, Jim Kirby, chair of the county commission, was enjoying his new role. He was no stranger to county government; he had been the minority commissioner for eight years under Republican administrations, but that, he felt, was essentially a "naysayer" role. Now, as chairman in a Democratic administration, he was in a position to take the lead on policy decisions, and he was enjoying it. He had founded a very successful business in the county and had called the shots there for more than thirty years. Although Kirby had often mused that government and business were much more different than alike—at least on paper—he relished his leadership role in the county.

Kirby prided himself on his capacity for work and made every effort to keep on top of things. He regretted that he had not read Goodheart's memorandum of April 5 before attending the monthly prison board meeting. He hated to be blind-sided! The president judge of common pleas court, Harvey Strickland, who was also president of the prison board, had shown Kirby his copy of the memorandum as well as a copy of Dexter's memorandum of March 12, which had prompted Goodheart's reply. Strickland had been his usual amiable self, but Kirby knew from long experience that with him, you worried not about what he said but about what he left unsaid. The fact that Strickland had brought the memorandums with him to the meeting and his oblique references to "those in this life who are penny-wise and pound-foolish" convinced Kirby that trouble was brewing.

As soon as Kirby got back to his office, he called George Truly, the county administrator, and asked him to stop by. Truly was the perfect balance to Kirby. Kirby was "born to lead"—an activist by nature, full of ideas and restless energy and impatient with detail. Truly, on the other hand, was a "doer." A professional administrator with substantial background in local government, he disliked the publicity and pressure of policy leadership, preferring instead the satisfaction that came from making policies work and seeing that services were delivered. The two men understood each other and had developed an effective working relationship. Neither one worried about the line between policy and administration; each one understood the overlap between the two activities and freely advised the other about county problems.

As Truly walked through the doorway, Kirby asked him, "Are you familiar with Don Dexter's memo of March 12 and Charlie Goodheart's reply?"

Truly said that he was and that he had already spoken to Dexter about them but that he had been too late.

"What do you mean, too late?" Kirby asked. "This thing looks to me like it can still be salvaged."

"Then," Truly replied, "I guess you haven't seen Don's memorandum of April 7."

April 7

TO: Charles R. Goodheart, Director of Corrections

FROM: Donald D. Dexter, Finance Director

SUBJECT: Your Evasive Memorandum of April 5

In a sincere effort to implement the county commissioners' directive establishing a countywide cost containment program, I wrote to you on March 12. In my memorandum, I asked you to provide me with a detailed justification for the current rate of overtime usage and your plans to keep such expenditures to an absolute minimum.

In reply, you gave me three pages of generalities and gratuitous comments. You're the prison expert, not me. If I had any good ideas on how you could run your operation more efficiently or economically, you can be sure I'd offer them. But as I see it, that's your job, not mine. My job is to see to the financial well-being of this county, and I can't do my job if I don't get cooperation. That's all I'm asking for—your cooperation in achieving the goals set for all of us by the county commissioners. Your knowledge of the Old Testament is doubtless better than mine, but I do know that the Pharaoh didn't pay overtime. As far as I am concerned, you can have all the straw you want, but cut down on the overtime.

cc: George S. Truly, County Administrator
      Frank Friendly, Personnel Director

The decision problem

After Kirby had finished reading Dexter's memo of April 7, he sighed wearily, laid it aside, looked up at Truly, and said, "I see what you mean. Any suggestions?"

Truly was a career administrator who had spent twenty-two years in a series of increasingly demanding city management jobs before being recruited by Kirby to serve as Franklin County administrator. He had been given carte blanche in the recruitment of his administrative staff, and he had picked, among others, Don Dexter. Dexter was extremely bright; he had been the controller for a large manufacturing firm in the county—quite an accomplishment for a man who was not yet thirty. "But," Truly reflected, "he's never swum in political waters before, and there's no question that he's in over his head."

As the two men reviewed the situation, they tried to define the problem specifically, to identify possible courses of action, and to anticipate the probable outcomes of those alternatives.

It was evident that whatever they did, they had to do it quickly. Strickland could not yet have seen Dexter's memorandum of April 7. If he had, he would have had it with him at the meeting, and he would not have been so affable.

The cost containment program was important to Kirby and the other Democrat on the county commission. It was probably their best hope of reelection. If they exempted the county prison from the program for fear of what the prison board might do, the program could be weakened throughout the county. After all, why should the other departments conform if the prison wasn't expected to do its part?

Under the county code, the prison board, not the county commission, was responsible for approving all prison-related expenditures. The board, with its Republican majority, could give Goodheart a blank check if it wanted to, and the commissioners would be able to do nothing about it. "Well, not exactly 'nothing,' " groused Kirby. "We could direct the county solicitor to sue the prison board, but because the president of the board is also the president judge, that's more of a theoretical than a practical remedy."

In fact, it was much more likely that the prison board would wind up suing the county commissioners. If the board alleged that an imminent threat to public safety was created by the refusal of the commissioners and their agents to fund the county prison adequately, it could bring an action *in mandamus*. In that event, the prison board would not be likely to limit the action to the question of prison overtime but would, in all likelihood, open a Pandora's box of problems. Goodheart had documented many of these problems in his memorandum of April 5, and that memo would probably be Exhibit A at a trial. Issues most likely to be litigated included the needs for adequate prison staffing levels, proactive strategies to combat the high rate of turnover, and higher salaries for correctional officers.

Kirby knew that if political warfare broke out, the Republicans would move quickly to seize the high ground. They would allege that the Democrats were jeopardizing the safety and tranquility of the community for the sake of a few paltry dollars. Kirby was too old a hand to suppose that arguments of efficiency and economy would carry any weight with the public in such a debate—especially if people were convinced that they were going to be murdered in their beds.

Because all the elected officials in the county were Republicans with the exception of Kirby and the other Democratic commissioner, they could really make things untenable. So far, the elected officials had been cooperating in the cost containment program. If, however, they chose to support the prison board in a confrontation with the commission, the cost containment program would be thoroughly scuttled.

"Don Dexter really put us in a box," remarked Kirby.

"Yes, but he's young and bright; he won't make the same mistake again," replied Truly.

"If the president judge gets him in his sights, he won't have the opportunity," observed Kirby solemnly.

"Funny thing," Kirby continued. "Don was right; that memorandum from Charlie was evasive, but Don should have known better than to say so. More than that, he shouldn't have written at all. In a situation like that, you go to see the guy. Writing is a very incomplete, very limited way to communicate. It's a lot easier to talk tough to your dictating machine than to an adversary. My rules have always been, never write a letter if you can avoid it, and never throw one away."

After almost an hour of discussion, the two men had identified five alternative approaches to the problem. Unfortunately, none of them was without risk.

1. Exempt the prison from the cost containment program. Under this alternative, Kirby would contact Strickland informally and intimate that the commission would not be unduly concerned if the prison did not achieve its cost containment objectives. The justification offered would be that as a public safety and law enforcement agency, the prison ought not be held to the same standard of cost reduction as other agencies, lest public safety suffer. The main problem with this approach was that party loyalty was paramount in this county, and Strickland was certain to share this information with the other elected officials, especially the district attorney and the sheriff, who headed justice system agencies. Once the commissioners had yielded on the prison, it would be difficult for them to hold the line on other justice system agencies, and the cost containment program would be seriously jeopardized. The result could be that the majority commissioners would be branded as weak men of little resolve, and that could have serious spillover effects in other areas.

2. Fund an in-depth study of the prison by a nationally recognized group specializing in corrections. Because this was a solution proposed by the director of corrections, it would most likely gain the acceptance of the prison board. Apart from the cost of such a study, which could be considerable, its recommendations were not likely to be favorable to the county administration. Through long experience, Kirby and Truly had come to believe that special

interest groups of whatever ilk rarely supported anything antithetical to their special interest. Worse yet, a comprehensive study might only document and verify the types of complaints that the director of corrections had been making for years. It was one thing to ignore his complaints; it would be something quite different were the county administration to ignore the studied recommendations of nationally recognized experts.

3. Conduct an in-house study of the need for prison overtime. This alternative appeared to have a good deal to recommend it. The county had a small management analysis team that reported directly to the county administrator. The supervisor of the team was a thoroughly honest and objective career professional who had been a founding member of the Association of Management Analysts in State and Local Government (MASLIG) and was well respected both within the county and beyond its borders. The problem, of course, was one of credibility. Despite his excellent reputation, his objectivity might be questioned in the partisan political climate that prevailed in Franklin County. Moreover, the prison board might refuse to approve such a study. A study could be undertaken without the prison board's concurrence, as a prerogative of the majority commissioners, but in that event, the prison board might view the study as flawed.

4. Attempt to find an "honest broker" to conduct a study of prison overtime. "Honest" in this context meant someone who would be considered honest in the eyes of the prison board—someone they would perceive as having no ax to grind. Ideally, this person should already work for the county and be known by, and enjoy the confidence of, the prison board. But who? The downside of this alternative, assuming that such a person could be found, was that the "honest broker" might not be all that honest. Should such a person be selected with the prison board's concurrence, that person might very well take the prison board's side, to the considerable embarrassment of the county administration.

5. Invite Strickland to undertake the overtime study with members of his staff. The court's administrative staff included several career professionals in court administration who were graduates of the Institute for Court Management. They were undoubtedly capable of conducting the study, and Strickland and the prison board, which he clearly dominated, would certainly find them acceptable. The question, again, was one of objectivity. Truly favored this alternative, arguing that if, as he believed, they were really professionals, they would be objective. Kirby's response was insightful: "I don't recall book and verse, but somewhere in the scripture it is written, 'Whose bread I eat, his song I sing,' and those fellows eat court bread."

What really was needed was a dispassionate review of prison overtime usage, the development of sound recommendations that would reduce overtime expenses without endangering the public, and an appraisal of the adequacy of the current budgetary allocation for prison overtime. This last point was particularly important. Goodheart continually reminded the prison board that his overtime request had been cut arbitrarily by the finance department without consultation or even explanation. True, there were other important questions that the study could appropriately consider, such as the adequacy of entry-level salaries for correctional officers and the appropriateness of current staffing levels. But solutions to both of these problems would be likely to cost the county more money. Given a choice, Kirby would prefer to postpone consideration of all problems that might result in increased cost to the county until after the next election.

Fortunately, the collective bargaining agreement with the local union that represented the correctional officers was due to expire in September. The study would certainly be completed well before then, and any recommendations requiring work-rule changes could be negotiated as part of the contract settlement.

Kirby turned to Truly and said, "George, give this some thought—and quickly! See what you can come up with."

Truly's recommendation was a combination of alternatives 3, 4, and 5. He saw no reason to exempt the prison from measures that applied to all other parts of the county government, and he believed that the only way to obtain data for an objective approach to the issue was to commission a study, preferably by an "honest broker." After considering and rejecting several possibilities, Truly recommended that a study be conducted by a team to be headed by Geraldine Eager, administrative assistant to the minority commissioner. Eager was the daughter of the county chair of the Republican Party. All of the Republican majority members of the prison board had known her since she was an infant, and all were beholden to her father. Eager had just completed her work for an M.P.A. degree and was looking forward to a career as a professional local government manager. She had interned in Truly's office, and he had established a mentoring relationship with her. She was relatively inexperienced, but that problem could be overcome by having the county's management analysis staff assist her in the study.

Kirby suggested the arrangement to minority Commissioner Joe Finley, Eager's boss. He felt reasonably certain that Finley would jump at the idea. Kirby knew that Finley had promised Eager's father to give Eager responsible work and that Finley had thus far been unable to deliver on that promise. Kirby also knew from his own experience that in the commission form of government, minority commissioners themselves have little challenging and responsible work to do.

Finley agreed to propose the arrangement to the prison board. The board concurred in the study plan, imposing the condition at Strickland's suggestion that a member of the court administrative staff be on the study team.

Truly met with Geraldine Eager to get the work underway. He described the problem at hand, explained the political complexities as well as the administrative sensitivities, and assured her that this assignment represented a major opportunity for her at this stage of her career. He gave her a list of the other members of the study team, told her that they had all received their letters of appointment, and asked her to convene a team meeting and get the project started as soon as possible. Finally, he gave her, in writing, the following specific charge: "The study team, under your leadership, is to

1. Gather the necessary data
2. Determine the adequacy of the overtime allocation made by the Finance Department
3. Suggest any and all ways in which prison overtime might be reduced without endangering the public safety
4. Prepare a staff presentation supportive of your findings and conclusions (such staff report should include your recommendations regarding implementation strategies)
5. Present your staff report and be prepared to defend it based upon your analysis of the data and your estimation of the political situation in which this problem has arisen."

Eager convened the study group, worked with it in compiling the needed data (presented here as Tables 1–4), and now is faced with the task of preparing a draft of a report responding to charges 2 through 5 for review by the study group.

She is anxious to find a solution to the problem, one that will be acceptable to Dexter, Goodheart, and Friendly, impress Truly and the county's political leadership, and dispel any rumors that her job may have been given to her because of her father rather than because of her ability. She must find a solution to the overtime problem.

(*continued on page 61*)

Table 1 Prison overtime hours (by cause or purpose within week, January 1–July 5)

Week	Vacation	Sick leave	Workmen's comp.	Holiday overtime	Resign. turnover	Medical leave	Unauth. absence	Add'l security req.[a]	Court appearances	Floor stripping	Jury duty	Hospital watch
01-Jan–04-Jan	8.00	56.00	8.00	501.50	—	—	—	11.25	—	—	—	16.00
05-Jan–11-Jan	—	48.00	87.25	—	8.00	—	—	3.00	—	—	—	8.00
12-Jan–18-Jan	15.00	91.50	40.00	—	—	—	—	10.00	—	—	—	8.00
19-Jan–25-Jan	16.00	102.50	—	633.25	—	—	—	—	—	—	—	—
26-Jan–01-Feb	8.00	112.50	8.00	—	—	—	—	0.25	—	—	—	—
02-Feb–08-Feb	16.00	72.50	16.00	—	—	—	24.00	11.25	—	—	—	46.00
09-Feb–15-Feb	—	87.25	40.00	—	—	—	32.00	45.50	—	—	—	—
16-Feb–22-Feb	—	104.00	88.25	599.75	—	—	16.00	1.25	—	—	—	0.75
23-Feb–01-Mar	16.00	71.00	37.00	—	—	—	34.00	—	2.00	—	40.00	—
02-Mar–08-Mar	—	42.00	96.00	—	64.00	—	—	12.00	—	—	—	—
09-Mar–15-Mar	7.50	151.50	72.00	—	24.00	—	16.25	15.00	1.00	—	—	292.25
16-Mar–22-Mar	8.00	59.75	24.00	—	24.00	—	—	32.00	—	—	—	24.00
23-Mar–29-Mar	15.75	112.00	47.75	585.00	72.00	—	—	0.25	—	—	—	—
30-Mar–05-Apr	8.00	24.00	56.00	—	40.00	16.00	—	14.25	—	—	—	—
06-Apr–12-Apr	16.00	48.00	13.00	—	64.00	—	—	61.00	—	—	—	95.50
13-Apr–19-Apr	—	71.50	32.00	—	63.50	7.75	24.00	0.50	—	—	—	72.00
20-Apr–26-Apr	8.00	72.00	24.00	—	40.00	8.00	16.00	25.25	—	—	—	8.50
27-Apr–03-May	—	148.25	32.00	—	24.00	—	—	53.00	—	104.50	—	120.00
04-May–10-May	8.00	79.00	82.50	—	49.50	—	11.75	66.75	1.75	52.50	—	118.00
11-May–17-May	6.00	59.25	43.00	—	79.00	24.00	7.50	16.50	7.75	6.50	—	68.00
18-May–24-May	48.00	89.75	67.50	—	88.00	24.00	—	57.50	—	2.00	—	53.75
25-May–31-May	24.00	98.25	56.00	513.50	34.50	8.00	17.25	17.75	—	—	—	16.00
01-Jun–07-Jun	8.00	64.00	56.00	—	54.00	—	14.50	26.25	—	—	—	—
08-Jun–14-Jun	56.00	120.25	55.00	623.25	64.00	—	14.00	21.25	1.00	—	—	126.00
15-Jun–21-Jun	88.00	162.00	16.00	—	168.00	8.00	24.50	43.25	1.75	—	—	—
22-Jun–28-Jun	36.25	191.25	—	—	140.00	8.00	—	39.00	10.25	—	—	—
29-Jun–05-Jul	—	176.50	—	515.75	88.00	32.00	—	30.50	—	—	—	30.50
Total	416.50	2,514.50	1,097.25	3,972.00	1,188.50	135.75	251.75	614.50	25.50	165.50	40.00	1,103.25
Rank order[b]	9	2	5	1	3	14	10	7	25	12	18	4

[a] Extra overtime due to shakedowns.
[b] Overtime categories ranked from 1 through 30 by total number of hours.

Table 1 (*continued*)

Week	Clerical duties	Lateness	Mental health hearing	Funeral leave	Maint. problems	Add'l duties in intake unit	Add'l duties in canteen	Misc. meetings	Completing reports	Employee review board	Military leave	Misc. office operation
01-Jan–04-Jan	8.75	—	3.75	—	—	—	—	—	—	—	—	—
05-Jan–11-Jan	10.50	—	—	14.25	3.00	1.50	1.00	2.25	4.75	3.25	—	0.50
12-Jan–18-Jan	6.50	0.75	—	1.75	—	—	0.50	—	0.75	—	—	—
19-Jan–25-Jan	3.50	0.25	—	—	—	—	2.00	—	—	—	—	—
26-Jan–01-Feb	10.50	0.25	—	—	6.00	—	—	—	1.00	1.00	8.00	—
02-Feb–08-Feb	4.50	6.25	2.50	—	2.00	—	1.75	—	1.00	—	8.00	—
09-Feb–15-Feb	4.00	0.25	—	—	16.50	—	1.00	9.50	0.50	—	—	—
16-Feb–22-Feb	1.25	0.50	—	—	5.50	—	6.00	3.00	—	—	—	—
23-Feb–01-Mar	1.50	0.25	4.75	—	2.50	—	3.50	—	—	—	—	—
02-Mar–08-Mar	—	—	1.50	—	2.75	—	2.25	1.00	2.75	—	—	—
09-Mar–15-Mar	—	1.50	—	—	2.25	—	3.75	—	—	—	8.00	—
16-Mar–22-Mar	—	0.25	—	—	—	—	2.25	2.00	—	—	—	—
23-Mar–29-Mar	—	—	—	8.00	—	—	1.50	4.00	—	—	—	—
30-Mar–05-Apr	2.00	5.00	3.25	—	1.75	—	1.25	—	—	—	—	—
06-Apr–12-Apr	—	1.00	3.25	—	1.25	—	3.00	—	1.25	—	—	—
13-Apr–19-Apr	—	1.25	1.25	8.00	—	—	—	—	—	—	8.00	8.00
20-Apr–26-Apr	—	—	—	—	—	—	—	—	—	—	—	—
27-Apr–03-May	—	8.00	—	—	—	—	2.50	—	—	—	8.00	1.50
04-May–10-May	—	1.75	—	—	7.50	—	—	—	—	—	8.00	—
11-May–17-May	—	—	—	—	0.50	—	—	5.75	2.25	23.00	8.00	8.00
18-May–24-May	0.50	1.50	—	—	—	—	—	14.50	0.50	—	8.00	8.00
25-May–31-May	—	0.50	1.00	—	—	2.50	—	—	2.50	—	—	8.00
01-Jun–07-Jun	—	2.25	—	—	5.50	—	—	—	—	—	8.00	—
08-Jun–14-Jun	—	3.25	—	—	—	—	—	13.50	3.00	—	—	0.50
15-Jun–21-Jun	—	0.50	—	—	—	—	—	—	0.50	1.50	—	—
22-Jun–28-Jun	—	2.75	—	—	—	—	—	—	1.00	—	24.00	—
29-Jun–05-Jul	—	0.75	—	—	—	—	—	—	2.00	—	70.00	—
Total	53.50	38.75	21.25	32.00	57.00	4.00	32.25	55.50	23.75	28.75	166.00	34.50
Rank order	17	19	26	23	15	30	22	16	26	24	11	21

Table 1 (*continued*)

Week	Leave of absence	Add'l duties in couns./treat.	Add'l duties in records off.	E.R.T. training & other	Add'l duties in sanitation	Misc. residual	Total non-holiday overtime	Total overtime
01-Jan–04-Jan	—	—	—	—	—	—	111.75	613.25
05-Jan–11-Jan	—	13.50	—	—	—	5.25	214.00	214.00
12-Jan–18-Jan	—	—	4.00	—	0.75	13.75	192.50	192.50
19-Jan–25-Jan	—	—	8.00	—	—	—	133.00	766.25
26-Jan–01-Feb	—	—	10.00	—	—	10.75	176.25	176.25
02-Feb–08-Feb	—	—	—	—	—	10.50	222.25	222.25
09-Feb–15-Feb	—	—	—	24.00	—	0.50	261.00	261.00
16-Feb–22-Feb	—	—	16.00	111.75	—	2.25	356.50	956.25
23-Feb–01-Mar	—	—	—	37.25	—	5.00	254.75	254.75
02-Mar–08-Mar	—	—	—	42.25	—	12.25	278.75	278.75
09-Mar–15-Mar	—	—	11.00	16.00	—	13.50	628.00	628.00
16-Mar–22-Mar	—	—	—	31.00	—	8.00	214.75	214.75
23-Mar–29-Mar	—	—	—	—	—	16.75	270.25	855.25
30-Mar–05-Apr	—	—	16.00	—	—	8.25	203.50	203.50
06-Apr–12-Apr	—	—	3.00	147.00	—	0.75	450.00	450.00
13-Apr–19-Apr	—	—	8.00	8.00	—	—	329.75	329.75
20-Apr–26-Apr	—	—	—	—	—	60.25	254.00	254.00
27-Apr–03-May	16.00	—	10.00	—	8.00	41.00	584.75	584.75
04-May–10-May	22.75	0.50	8.00	128.00	—	37.50	675.75	675.75
11-May–17-May	—	1.00	10.00	16.00	—	29.00	422.00	422.00
18-May–24-May	—	0.50	8.00	60.50	—	8.00	499.00	499.00
25-May–31-May	—	—	—	4.50	—	36.50	351.75	865.25
01-Jun–07-Jun	—	—	8.00	—	4.00	8.75	275.25	275.25
08-Jun–14-Jun	—	—	—	40.00	—	29.50	499.25	1,122.50
15-Jun–21-Jun	—	2.50	15.00	16.00	—	34.00	549.50	549.50
22-Jun–28-Jun	—	—	11.00	40.50	—	6.00	561.75	561.75
29-Jun–05-Jul	—	—	8.50	73.50	—	24.00	572.50	1,088.25
Total	38.75	18.00	154.50	796.25	12.75	422.00	9,542.50	13,514.50
Rank order	19	28	13	6	29	8		

Table 2   Shift staffing schedule

Post	1st shift[a] position(s)[b]	Factor[c]	2nd shift position(s)	Factor	3rd shift position(s)	Factor	Totals position(s)	Factor
Module A	1	1.67	1	1.67	1	1.66	3	5.00
Module B	1	1.67	1	1.67	1	1.66	3	5.00
Module C	1	1.67	1	1.67	1	1.66	3	5.00
Module D	1	1.67	1	1.67	1	1.66	3	5.00
Module E	1	1.67	1	1.67	1	1.66	3	5.00
Module F	1	1.67	1	1.67	1	1.66	3	5.00
Module G	1	1.67	1	1.67	1	1.66	3	5.00
Module H	1	1.67	1	1.67	1	1.66	3	5.00
MHU	1	1.67	1	1.67	1	1.66	3	5.00
RHU	1	1.67	1	1.67	1	1.66	3	5.00
Main control	1	1.67	1	1.67	1	1.66	3	5.00
Housing control	1	1.67	1	1.67	1	1.66	3	5.00
Outer perimeter	1	1.20					1	1.20
Medical dispensary	1	1.67	1	1.67			2	3.34
Transportation	2	2.40					2	2.40
Public entrance	1	1.67	1	1.67			2	3.34
Reception unit	2	3.34	2	3.34	1	1.66	5	8.34
Canteen	1	1.20					1	1.20
Warehouse key cont.	1	1.20					1	1.20
Sanitation	2	2.40	1	1.20			3	3.60
Laundry	1	1.20					1	1.20
Special assignment	7	11.69	7	11.69	2	3.32	16	26.70
Recep. supervisor	1	1.00					1	1.00
Sergeant	2	3.34	2	3.34	1	1.66	5	8.34
Lieutenant	1	1.67	1	1.67	1	1.66	3	5.00
Training Lt.	1	1.00					1	1.00
Captain	1	1.00					1	1.00
Deputy warden (S)	1	1.00					1	1.00
Dietary (CO)	2	3.34	2	3.34			4	6.68
Dietary super.	1	1.00					1	1.00
Maintenance	3	3.00					3	3.00
Maintenance super.	1	1.00					1	1.00
Deputy warden (O)	1	1.00					1	1.00
Records clk.-typ.	2	2.00	1	1.00			3	3.00
Records super.	1	1.00					1	1.00
Treatment housing	5	6.00					5	6.00
Treatment intake	1	1.67	1	1.67			2	3.34
Operations clerk-sten.	1	1.00					1	1.00
Records officer (CO)	1	1.00	1	1.00			2	2.00
Associate warden	1	1.00					1	1.00
Librarian	1	1.00					1	1.00
D/A clerk-typist	1	1.00					1	1.00
D/A supervisor	1	1.00					1	1.00
Treatment clerk-typist	1	1.00					1	1.00
C/S bookkeeper	1	1.00					1	1.00
C/S director	1	1.00					1	1.00
Deputy warden (T)	1	1.00					1	1.00
Bus. bookkeeper	2	2.00					2	2.00
Bus. clerk-typist	1	1.00					1	1.00
Asst. bus. manager	1	1.00					1	1.00
Business manager	1	1.00					1	1.00
Admin. aide	1	1.00					1	1.00
Admin. assistant	1	1.00					1	1.00
Sec'y to warden	1	1.00					1	1.00
Warden	1	1.00					1	1.00
Totals							123	175.88

[a] The first shift is the day shift; the second is the evening shift; the third is the night shift.
[b] *Position(s)* refers to the number of persons who must be on duty in the prison during the shift to meet the requirements for staffing this position.
[c] *Factor* refers to the number of persons who must be employed by the prison to assure the availability of sufficient staff to meet the staffing level for this position on an everyday basis.

Table 3   Average hourly rates and prison staffing plan[a]

Job title	Number of positions	Average hourly rate
Operations		
Director of corrections	1	$21.15
Assistant warden	1	18.03
Deputy warden	3	14.87
Captain of security	1	13.55
Lieutenant—corrections	6	11.64
Sergeant—corrections	10	9.82
Corrections officer	110	7.35
Staff and service		
Assistant business manager	1	$8.90
Corrections officer—maintenance	3	10.60
D/A supervisor	1	10.94
Fiscal plans officer	1	12.07
Bookkeeper	5	7.12
Librarian	1	8.66
Administrative aide	1	8.01
Assistant to Dir. of corrections	1	11.56
Coordinator of volunteers	1	11.96
Building systems supervisor	1	14.43
Cook	8	7.32
Secretary	1	7.70
Clerk-stenographer	1	7.12
Clerk-typist	8	6.54
Doctor	2	11.10
Counselor	9	9.08
Total	177[b]	

[a] Computed from county payroll records of July 5.
[b] Total authorized positions = 181, 4 positions vacant as of July 5.

Table 4   Prision budget request and finance department allocation for overtime

Type of overtime	Prison budget request	Finance dept. allocation	Difference
Holiday	$188,365	$188,365	$ 0
Non-holiday	$264,002	$130,635	($115,367)
Total	$434,367	$319,000	($115,367)

Discussion questions

1. Judging from the statements and actions of the principal actors in the case, in what ways did their value premises differ?
2. What purposes, if any, are served by ''going on record,'' as Dexter did in his first memorandum?
3. Instead of dictating his reply to Goodheart's memorandum of April 5 while he was still angry, what should Dexter have done?
4. Was Kirby correct in his observation that ''writing is a very incomplete, very limited way to communicate''?
5. Are Kirby's and Truly's reservations about the objectivity of a nationally recognized group of corrections experts well founded? Would the recommendations of such a group be more likely to support or oppose the director of corrections? Why?

6. What would represent a reasonable overtime budget for the department? What calculations are needed to arrive at such a figure?

7. If you were Geraldine Eager, what solution would you recommend to the study group as a basis for its discussion? (Alternatively, if the response to these questions is part of a group project, what would your group recommend to Truly as a solution to the problem?)

8. What political reaction might be expected to the group's proposal? What, if any, responses should the group be prepared to make to such reactions?

6 Managing debt and the capital budget

Editor's introduction

Developing and implementing an annual operating budget is a standard procedure in governments utilizing the good management practices developed during the twentieth century government reform movement. Capital budgeting, or the development of a multi-year plan for major expenditures, is another of the reform movement's good management practices, but it is utilized much less frequently. Many governments, including the federal and many state governments, finance capital expenditures on a pay-as-you-go basis, but most local governments find it difficult to generate the large, up-front sums of cash needed to pay for capital expenditures, and especially for infrastructure development.

Thus, capital budgeting is undertaken in most well-managed local governments. It involves advance planning, usually projecting at least five or six years into the future, for capital expenditure needs; prioritizing such needs; and then developing a strategy to pay for the planned acquisitions. Out of either necessity or strategic choice, governments often borrow as a means of financing capital expenditures.

This case, "Infrastructure Demands versus Debt," describes such a process, focusing particularly on the tough policy questions relating to capital financing. It describes the development of the capital budget; portrays the options for obtaining the money needed to implement the budget, including the advantages and disadvantages of each option; and sets forth the kinds of data to be analyzed in the process of selecting a financing option.

In the process, the case introduces the reader to some key policy elements inherent in the task of debt management. It describes the linkage between capital expenditure needs, annual appropriations, and debt service costs. It introduces the problem of statutory debt limitations and reflects on the policy implications of pay-as-you-go, short-term borrowing, and long-term borrowing strategies. It highlights the importance of debt management expertise in the portfolio of skills possessed by the local government manager and finance officer.

This case also explores the relationships among capital budgeting, capital financing, and the community's political environment. Capital planning and debt management, like all other parts of the local government management challenge, are bounded by the political "art of the possible." In the case at hand, Manager Harper knows that not only his own job, but the credibility of professional management in Clearview, is at risk in the capital financing decisions he must make.

Capital financing and debt management, then, provide one more forum in which the abilities of the local government manager/finance officer are tested. But, as is clearly evident in this case, they provide yet another opportunity—and a major opportunity—to build a better community and improve the quality of life for its residents. And that, in the final analysis, is the ultimate purpose of professional local government management.

Case 6
Infrastructure demands versus debt

J. Peter Braun

Background

Bill Harper is the newly appointed manager in Clearview Township. Named to the job after an eight-month vacancy in the manager's position, Bill is a professional local government manager. Following a college career in which he earned under-graduate and graduate degrees in political science and public administration, he served in various professional management capacities in three communities before assuming his duties in Clearview at age 32.

Harper's new community, Clearview, is a suburb of 25,000 people located in the New York metropolitan region. A small, rural town for many years, it has exploded with new growth during the past decade. This growth has generated a tremendous increase in both the need and the demand for more public services, for expansion to and improvement of existing infrastructure, and for new facilities.

These growing pains have caused considerable turmoil and political activism in Clearview, much of it centered around the public's demands for more services, on the one hand, and its resistance to higher taxes, on the other hand. To make matters worse, neither the manager's job nor the town's commitment to council-manager government is secure.

The municipal government

Largely because of the growth of the past decade, Clearview changed from a cen-tury-old "committee" form of government to the council-manager form three years ago. The change in the form of government was approved in a public referendum, based on the recommendation of a citizens' charter study commission appointed under the state's Optional Charter Law for Local Government. The impetus for establishment of the charter study commission had been a widespread dissatisfac-tion with the level and quality of public services in Clearview.

As is frequently the case, the existing power structure opposed the change in the form of government, and two of its members were elected to the first five-member council under the council-manager form.

The first manager appointee under the new system, Richard Wentz, was bright and well educated but inexperienced. One of the primary reasons for his appoint-ment was to satisfy pressures to pay a relatively small salary. The township council wanted to offset the criticism, by those opposed to the change in form of govern-ment, of having a "high-priced outsider" appointed to the new position. Wentz resigned under pressure after only six months in office.

In seeking a replacement, the township council gave priority to appointing a person with at least ten years' municipal government experience. Robert Taylor was the person selected. Taylor was also professionally qualified and met the ex-perience criterion established by the council. However, he too faced difficulties, including allegations of lacking strong work habits, and he was dismissed from office after two years.

The dismissal of Robert Taylor occurred three months before the biennial mu-nicipal election, which resulted in a new 4-to-3 partisan majority on the council. Fortunately, all members of the council pledged to work together for the improve-ment of the community.

Bill Harper was unanimously appointed by the council and charged with the task of providing strong management to the community. Specifically, he was directed to improve operating efficiency and to respond to the public demand for new and better services. As the mayor said to Harper, "I think we have about two years to establish credibility with the public, or you will see a new push to change the council-manager form of government."

Immediate challenges

Clearview's population had doubled in the past decade. The old, informal committee form of government simply had been unable to increase public services to cope with this growth. The police department was the largest and strongest department in the municipal government. The chief of police and township clerk were the two senior employees; both had a high level of influence in local government activities. The public works department had good personnel but lacked professional leadership and supervision. Virtually all other services, including engineering, planning, construction inspection, and recreation, were provided by part-time personnel.

When Harper arrived in Clearview, he found no systematic program for road improvements, stormwater drainage, and other types of infrastructure development. The township owned no parkland other than a single tract that had been donated as an open-space preserve by a philanthropic landowner in the community. Virtually the only road improvements completed in the past ten years had been a haphazard surge of road resurfacing just before the last election in an attempt to assuage Clearview's residents. One small road reconstruction project undertaken at the same time proved disastrous due to lack of leadership in the public works department: nearly all personnel were assigned to the reconstruction project, with no one left available to handle service requests, citizen complaints, and day-to-day activities for more than six weeks.

During his first year as manager, Harper gave priority to establishing improved operating systems and to obtaining qualified, professional personnel for major township positions. A totally new budget format was established, a six-year capital improvement program was prepared for the first time, and formal personnel and purchasing procedures were written. With the strong support of the council, Harper appointed a full-time engineer, planner, health officer, tax assessor, and director of parks and recreation. All of the new appointees were well-qualified professionals recruited from outside the township. Some undercurrents began to develop in the political community about "Harper's Empire," and the time pressure mounted to demonstrate the benefit of the new staff in terms of improved services and infrastructure.

The case

After attending to the immediate problem of staffing and operational systems, Harper was faced with the financial management problem of planning and accomplishing much-needed infrastructure and other capital improvements.

Already a challenging problem of financial management, the task was made more difficult both by the "Harper's Empire" attitude held by some old-line politicians and by the antitax/smaller-government philosophy generally prevalent in the region. The problem was further complicated by the need to address the consequences of the town's failure to invest in capital improvements during the previous ten years of rapid population growth.

On the positive side, Clearview was a burgeoning community and had the benefit of an expanding real estate tax base from new development. Also, the same neglect as prevailed toward capital improvements existed toward the process of reviewing township fees for services. Thus, it was possible to increase revenues on a reasonable basis by playing "catch-up" on fees that had not been adjusted for many years.

The most important "catch-up" fees were filing fees for development applications, building permits, and engineering inspection services. Based on the town's rapid growth and on the new rates established, revenues from these sources almost doubled over three years, increasing from approximately $270,000 to about $500,000. This was a substantial increase in revenue, but total fees of $500,000 per year still only represented 2.5 percent of Clearview's $20 million budget. Essentially, the fee increases offset salaries for the new professional personnel hired during Harper's first year in Clearview.

Preparing the capital budget

As a basis for capital improvement planning, Harper established a formal capital budgeting process. All department heads were invited to submit six-year capital improvement requests. Immediate funding of 51 projects was requested for the forthcoming year, at a total cost of more than $2.8 million. This figure dwarfed prior capital appropriations in the annual budget, which had amounted to $100,000 or less.

More important, the original six-year program included more than 110 projects, with a total estimated cost of $11.5 million. These capital improvement needs covered the gamut of the demands of municipal activity, including fire equipment, road resurfacing and other infrastructure improvements, and parks and recreation facilities. The capital requests submitted for the six-year capital improvement program are shown in Table 1, pages 67–70. This tabulation was, by far, the most comprehensive listing of capital improvement needs that had ever been prepared in the township.

In addition, the township recently had taken over an independent water and sewer authority. The former authority, carrying a total debt of some $16 million, had pending projects, including a major sewer extension, with an estimated cost of $3.5 million. Although funding for water and sewer improvements was provided by utility fees and revenues, the indebtedness for water and sewer facilities had to be considered and incorporated within the overall debt limitations of the township.

Prioritization of capital improvements

Harper asked the planning board to form a four-member subcommittee to work with him annually in identifying priorities among capital budget requests, as part of an ongoing process of updating the six-year capital improvement program. When all capital improvement requests had been compiled, this capital budget subcommittee met with Harper and applied a weighted ranking system to all projects requested in the first year. Fortunately, the four members of the capital budget subcommittee provided a representative mix of views that resulted in a good balance of priorities for funding in the annual budget.

The first-year capital improvement requests are listed in their prioritized order in Table 2. Heading the list was a $100,000 payment to the township's capital improvement reserve; this continued a township practice of supplementing its annual capital expenditure appropriation with an additional payment of $100,000 to a capital improvement reserve, from which capital expenses were covered on an as-needed basis.

As part of his first capital improvement program, Harper set a goal of increasing annual cash appropriations for capital improvements to a minimum of $400,000 per year. He also proposed a bonded indebtedness of $2.5 million for the forthcoming fiscal year to fund an immediate, major increase in capital improvements.

The recommendations both for cash appropriations and for new indebtedness were based on the staff's analysis of current budget data and on an analysis of the statutory debt limitation of the township. These analyses are summarized in Tables 3 and 4.

(*continued on page 71*)

Table 1 Tabulation of capital program requests and funding summary

Tabulation of requests

Department	Project	Total estimated cost	Prior appropriation	CFY + 1	CFY + 2	CFY + 3	CFY + 4	CFY + 5	CFY + 6	Later
General government	Computer equipment	$ 50,000		$ 50,000						
	Reserve for administrative vehicles	350,000		50,000	$ 50,000	$ 50,000	$ 50,000	$ 50,000	$ 50,000	$ 50,000
Fire	Aerial truck/renovation	350,000	$19,000					331,000		
	Replace '82 E-One (32–31)	235,000		235,000						
	Pagers/radios	30,000		5,000	5,000	5,000	5,000	5,000	5,000	
	Upgrade personal protection and safety equipment	60,000		10,000	10,000	10,000	10,000	10,000	10,000	
	Replace hose	24,000		4,000	4,000	4,000	4,000	4,000	4,000	
	Exhaust system—4 firehouses	70,000		70,000						
	Office renovation	20,000		20,000						
	Replace '83 3-D (32–51)	235,000			235,000					
	Fire support vehicle	235,000				235,000				
	Replace '90 Suburban	45,000						45,000		
	Replace fire official's '91 Caprice	20,000							20,000	
	Upgrade communication system	150,000						150,000		
Rescue	Replace vehicle 32–91	72,000			72,000					
	Replace vehicle 32–93	75,000				75,000				
	Pager replacement	2,500		2,500						
	Turnout gear	10,000		10,000						
	1st Response vehicle replacement	25,000			25,000					
Police	Radio replacement	45,500		6,500	6,500	6,500	6,500	6,500	6,500	
	Reserve-vehicle equipment	35,000		5,000	5,000	5,000	5,000	5,000	5,000	
	Bulletproof vest replacement	21,000		3,000	3,000	3,000	3,000	3,000	3,000	
	Reserve weapons	21,000		3,000	3,000	3,000	3,000	3,000	3,000	
	Police computer replacement	70,000		10,000	10,000	10,000	10,000	10,000	10,000	
	Replace photocopier	12,000		12,000						
Public works	Road resurfacing	2,695,000		325,000	345,000	365,000	385,000	405,000	425,000	445,000
	Replace pickup truck #907	20,000		20,000						
	Replace dump truck #913	41,900		41,900						
	Replace loader #932	94,000		94,000						

(continued on page 68)

Table 1   (*continued from page 67*)

Tabulation of requests

Department	Project	Total estimated cost	Prior appropriation	CFY + 1	CFY + 2	CFY + 3	CFY + 4	CFY + 5	CFY + 6	Later
	Replace plow set-up	37,500		5,500	5,800	6,100	6,400	6,700	7,000	
	Replace loader/backhoe #934	57,200		57,200						
	Replace 1.5-ton roller #936	14,700		14,700						
	Purchase mig welder	2,600		2,600						
	Replace radio equipment	29,400		4,400	4,600	4,800	5,000	5,200	5,400	
	Paint exterior of township garage	2,100		2,100						
	Replace doors of township garage	4,500		4,500						
	Purchase vertical trench shore system	4,100		4,100						
	Replace utility truck #781	19,500		19,500						
	Replace generator at Shongum Pumping Station	15,000		15,000						
	Purchase generator for County College Pumping Station	15,000		15,000						
	Purchase comminutor for Shongum Pumping Station	10,000		10,000						
	Replace 3'-diaphragm pump	1,500		1,500						
	Replace utility truck #901	25,400						25,400		
	Replace pickup truck #902	23,100					23,100			
	Replace pickup truck #903	21,000			21,000					
	Replace pickup truck #904	21,000			21,000					
	Replace pickup truck #905	21,000			21,000					
	Replace pickup truck #908	21,000			21,000					
	Replace dump truck #911	41,500				41,500				
	Replace dump truck #914	50,900			50,900					
	Replace sanding truck #923	153,800				153,800				
	Replace sanding truck #924	153,800				153,800				
	Replace sanding truck #925	161,400					161,400			
	Replace tractor/mower #937	50,000			50,000					
	Replace recycling truck #951	30,500			30,500					
	Replace brush shredder #962	62,400					62,400			
	Replace sweeper #972	233,500						233,500		
	Replace line striper #984	26,500					26,500			
	Replace pressure washer #988	6,500							6,500	
	Replace pickup truck #782	17,000				17,000				
	Replace van #783	19,100							19,100	
	Replace pickup truck #784	17,000			17,000					

	Item	Amount					
	Replace pickup truck #785	23,300			23,300		
	Replace air compressor #791	14,000		14,000	14,000		
	Replace confined-space equipment	13,400	13,400		13,400		
	Replace leak detector	3,000			3,000		
	Replace line tracer	4,000			4,000		
Parks,	New pickup truck	11,500			11,500		
recreation	Ford tractor replacement 4WD	14,000			14,000		
and	Park improvements, Stoney Brook	35,000			35,000		
community	Senior community center improvements	15,000		5,000	5,000		
affairs	Weed control, Randolph Park	7,000			7,000		
	Heistein parking repair and net	12,000			12,000		
	Replace pickup R-57 4WD	18,500			18,500		
	Brundage and Heistein Park bleachers	12,000		4,000	4,000		
	Randolph Park beach sand	21,000		3,000	3,000	3,000	3,000
	Replace Toro Field Pro	9,000					
	Replace mobile radios	3,000					
	Replace '85 Carmate trailer	6,500					
	New flammables storage cabinet	3,500					
	Brundage maintenance building expansion	25,000		25,000			
	New power washer for equipment	1,800			1,800		
	Brundage upgrade field lights	35,000			35,000		
	Randolph Park ADA upgrade and bleachers	11,500		3,500	8,000		
	Brundage bungalow repair	75,000			75,000		
	Heistein Park expansion	10,000			10,000		
	Toro Grounds Master	9,500			9,500		
	Snow blower	2,200			2,200		
	Sand volleyball courts, Brundage	4,000		4,000	4,000		
	Repave Heistein parking and lot	39,000		39,000			
	1988 Ford Transette seniors' bus	45,000		45,000			
	Backstop replacement, 4 fields	8,000	4,000	4,000			
	Brundage repave road	17,000			17,000		
	Millbrook tennis court repair	50,000			50,000		
	Heistein pavilion expansion and repair	15,000			15,000		
	Replace Gandy spreader	2,900			2,900		
	Replace Gravely tractor	3,900			3,900		

(continued on page 70)

Table 1 (continued from page 69)

Tabulation of requests

Department	Project	Total estimated cost	Prior appropriation	CFY + 1	CFY + 2	CFY + 3	CFY + 4	CFY + 5	CFY + 6	Later
	Heistein fencing upgrade	6,000						6,000		
	Heistein rip-rap stream area	25,000						25,000		
	Replace turf aerator	4,000				4,000				
	Upgrade mini-parks	8,000						8,000		
	Pool and recreation center development	3,000,000		1,500,000	1,500,000					
	Carmate trailer replacement	4,300			4,300					
	Replace power seeder	2,900							2,900	
	Brundage curb inner loop	45,000								45,000
	1994 seniors' bus	90,000								90,000
	Theater building addition	200,000			200,000					
	Replace various equipment	100,000							50,000	50,000
	Ice rink development	750,000								750,000
Library	Public-access computers	14,000		14,000						
Planning	Town center improvements	118,500		2,000	75,000	1,500	40,000			
	Bikeway	15,100		15,100						
Landmarks committee	Bungalow #4 restoration	23,348		23,348						
	Total	$11,470,048	$19,000	$2,856,248	$2,985,600	$1,257,500	$902,100	$1,353,700	$635,400	$1,460,500

Funding summary

Sources			CFY + 1	CFY + 2	CFY + 3	CFY + 4	CFY + 5	CFY + 6	Later
Current revenues		$ 1,823,418	$ 506,648	$ 414,700	$ 204,000	$231,770	$ 172,800	$148,500	$ 145,000
General obligation bonds or notes		9,066,700	2,281,200	2,427,000	982,600	546,400	1,119,500	425,000	1,285,000
Revenue bonds		0							
Special assessment bonds		0							
Capital improvements reserve		578,430	87,400	143,900	69,400	123,930	61,400	61,900	30,500
Grants-in-aid		1,500			1,500				
Private or other sources		0							
Total funding		$11,470,048	$2,875,248	$2,985,600	$1,257,500	$902,100	$1,353,700	$635,400	$1,460,500

Note: "CFY" refers to current fiscal year. The plus or minus number refers to the number of future or past years, respectively, from the current fiscal year. Thus "CFY+1" refers to "Current Fiscal Year plus one," or the next fiscal year.

As noted in Table 3, the township was fortunate in having a very large debt capacity under the law. This capacity partly reflected the lack of capital improvements in previous years, but it also highlighted the question of determining a critical balance: urgent capital improvement needs had to be met while keeping costs, and thus tax rates, within the range that the tax-resistant community had come to expect as a result of past decisions postponing expenditures. Table 3 shows Clearview's current debt, as well as the maximum borrowing capacity of the township that legally remains available for use on future projects.

Table 4 provides further data that were used to estimate the capital improvement strategy in the budget proposal for the forthcoming fiscal year.

Future growth

Continued rapid growth of Clearview was another crucial factor affecting capital improvement and financing decisions. During the five years preceding the fiscal year of the case study (CFY), 1,150 new homes had been constructed throughout the 21-square-mile municipality. This burst of construction resulted in an additional 28 miles of local streets and all of the service needs ensuing from an estimated population increase of some 4,000 persons. Although Clearview already was a primarily residential community, one good point about the recent residential de-

Table 2   Projects included in the capital budget with assigned priority ratings

Priority ranking	Description of item	CFY + 1 capital appropriation budget
1	Capital improvement reserve	$ 100,000
2	Road resurfacing	325,000
3	Rescue squad turnout gear	10,000
4	Replace 82 E-One (32–31), fire department	235,000
5	Fire department personal protection equipment	10,000
6	Police bulletproof vest replacement	3,000
7	Replace pickup truck #907 (DPW)	20,000
8	Police reserve weapons	3,000
9	Fire department—replace hoses	4,000
10	Police—replace photocopier	12,000
11	Replace generator at Shongum Pumping Station (DPW)	15,000
12	Computer equipment	50,000
13	Fire department—pagers/radios	5,000
14	Police radio replacement	6,500
15	Parks and recreation—replace Ford tractor 4WD	14,000
16	Replace 1.5-ton roller #936 (DPW)	14,700
17	Replace dump truck #913 (DPW)	41,900
18	Replace loader/backhoe #934 (DPW)	57,200
19	Purchase generator for CCM pumping station (DPW)	15,000
20	Police computer equipment	10,000
21	Replace plow setup (DPW)	5,500
22	Purchase comminutor for Shongum Station (DPW)	10,000
23	Replace loader #932 (DPW)	94,000
24	Rescue pager replacement	2,500
25	Reserve for administrative vehicles	50,000
26	Parks and recreation—senior community center improvements	5,000
27	Parks and recreation—replace Toro Field Pro	9,000
28	Parks and recreation—Randolph Park beach sand	3,000
29	Parks and recreation—new flammables storage cabinet	3,500

(*continued on page 72*)

Table 2 (*continued*)

Priority ranking	Description of item	CFY + 1 capital appropriation budget
30	Parks and recreation—weed control, Randolph Park	7,000
31	Planning and development—streetscape, town center	2,000
32	Police—reserve vehicle equipment	5,000
33	Replace utility truck #781 (DPW)	19,500
34	Parks and recreation—new pickup truck	11,500
35	Parks and recreation—replacement pickup truck R-57 4WD	18,500
36	Parks and recreation—bleachers at Brundage and Heistein Parks	4,000
37	Library—public-access terminals	14,000
38	Replace radio equipment (DPW)	4,400
39	Replace 3″-diaphragm pump (DPW)	1,500
40	Purchase mig welder (DPW)	2,600
41	Parks and recreation—replace mobile radios	3,000
42	Parks and recreation—improvements at Stoney Brook	35,000
43	Parks and recreation—replace '85 Carmate trailer	6,500
44	Parks and recreation—Heistein parking repair	12,000
45	Purchase vertical trench shore system	4,100
46	Fire department exhaust system (4 firehouses)	70,000
47	Fire department office renovation	20,000
48	Replacement of garage doors (DPW)	4,500
49	Paint exterior of township garage (DPW)	2,100
50	Parks and recreation—new power washer for equipment	1,800
51	Planning and development—bikeway	15,100
52	Parks and recreation—Brundage field lights	35,000
53	Parks and recreation—pool and recreation center development	1,500,000
54	Landmarks committee—Bungalow #4 restoration	23,348
	Total	$2,956,248

Note: "CFY" refers to current fiscal year. Thus, "CFY + 1"
refers to current fiscal year plus one, or the next fiscal year.

Table 3 Debt-incurring capacity

CFY − 2 state equalized value	$1,647,107,397
CFY − 1 state equalized value	1,652,625,222
CFY state equalized value	1,697,846,602
Equalized valuation basis	1,665,859,740

Average state valuation (CFY − 2, CFY − 1, and CFY)[a]	$1,665,859,740
Municipal 3.5% borrowing margin	58,305,091
Debt issued or authorized as of Dec. 31, CFY	14,854,000
Anticipated debt to be authorized in CFY + 1	500,000
Less debt to be retired in CFY + 2	1,009,200
Available borrowing authority (Jan. 1, CFY + 1)	41,941,891
Estimated debt to be authorized per capital budget	[b]

Board of education:	
School borrowing margin of 4%	$66,634,390
Debt issued and authorized Jan. 1, CFY	11,960,000
Debt to be retired (CFY + 1)	825,000
Available borrowing authority	53,849,390
Debt to be authorized per capital budget	0

[a] "CFY" refers to current fiscal year. The plus or minus number refers to the number of future or past years, respectively, from the current fiscal year.
[b] To be determined as part of the decision problem.

velopment boom was that new homes came in overwhelmingly at the higher range of sales prices, selling for an average of $450,000 or more. This trend continued despite a recent recession and Clearview's overall character as a middle-income community with a broad mix of housing alternatives. The advantage of this high-priced housing, coupled with the trend toward smaller family size, was that the additional tax revenues generated by new residential construction nearly equaled the extra costs of providing public services, particularly municipal services, to the new residents.

Because the trend in new construction was projected to continue, Clearview could count on some modest revenue growth to help support its capital budget expenditures.

Implementation of the capital program

The township council approved Harper's recommendations, although the goal of providing annual cash appropriations of $400,000 for capital improvements was amended to provide for annual increments of $100,000 each year until the goal was met. This meant that only $200,000 would be available for the first year of the capital improvement program.

The council also decided to fund the $2.5 million of bonded indebtedness by the use of temporary, short-term bond anticipation notes. A decision on permanent funding was postponed, but either cash appropriations or long-term financing ultimately would be needed. Both financing mechanisms would have to be coordinated with existing township and tax policies.

The new council, which had appointed Harper, increased Clearview's property tax levy during its first year to establish a "floor" of minimum service delivery. Because of this rise, Harper and the council found it possible to implement the new capital improvement program in the second year without a further tax increase.

Table 4 Guidelines for estimating capital improvement section of annual CFY + 1 budget

Item Year[a]	CFY − 4	CFY − 3	CFY − 2	CFY − 1	CFY	CFY + 1[b]
Capital improvement	$ 358,000	$ 278,000	$ 185,700	$ 367,248[c]	$ 370,654[c]	$ 400,000
Total operations budget[d]	$10,309,866	$10,271,922	$10,719,398	$ 11,391,534	$ 15,727,596	
Percentage of operations budget	3.5%	2.7%	1.7%	3.2%	2.4%	
Total general appropriations	$13,686,268	$14,007,539	$14,637,277	$ 15,378,944	$ 19,676,821	$21,703,534
Percentage of general appropriations	2.6%	2.0%	1.3%	2.4%	1.9%	1.8%

Increase in general appropriations

CFY − 4	12.3%
CFY − 3	2.3
CFY − 2	4.5
CFY − 1	5.1
CFY	27.9[e]
	52.1%

[a] "CFY" refers to current fiscal year. The plus or minus number refers to the number of future or past years, respectively, from the current fiscal year.
[b] All figures are projections.
[c] Capital improvement appropriation for these years includes reserve for open-space acquisition: $167,000 (CFY − 1) and $180,000 (CFY).

[d] This figure equals the general appropriations minus: capital improvements, debt service, deferred and statutory charges, and reserves for uncollected taxes.
[e] Percentage increase is greater in CFY due to the addition of water and sewer operations to the township budget.

The decision problem

During the process of appointing Harper as manager, the township council had communicated Clearview's needs. On his arrival in Clearview, Harper quickly recognized these needs at first hand. He moved first to provide professional staff commensurate with the needs of the community. At the same time, he established standard procedures and systems for day-to-day operations. These were all beneficial moves for the township, but they also represented rapid change within the organization. Harper recognized the undercurrent that had developed about the "new guy" bringing in all these outsiders and making all of these changes. In some cases, clear resistance arose against his proposals.

The staffing and procedural changes, however, had only set the stage. Now, action was needed to produce the actual services and facilities required to improve the quality of life in Clearview. Harper had managed to finance one year's component of the capital improvement budget, but short-term financing had been used, and there were still five more years to go. He now faced a dilemma: "How could I (1) continue to finance capital improvement needs quickly without building more resistance to higher taxes while (2) also providing the best long-range financial structure for the community?"

Not all of the pressures caused by new debt and debt service costs could be attributed to Harper's work. One of the problems that Harper and the new council inherited was a significant increase in debt for public improvements authorized by the prior council in an attempt to gain support for its members in the last municipal election. This debt included funding for water lines, road improvements, and construction of the township's first new municipal building. All of these improvements were funded by bond issues with a life of at least ten years. Table 5 summarizes in detail the debt inherited by Harper, together with the current annual debt-service costs that had to be paid from current revenues.

Harper knew that he must develop a strategy that would meet four objectives: (1) to provide for repayment of all of the outstanding past debt; (2) to make some provision to retire the $2.5 million in short-term debt authorized to cover capital expenditures in the coming fiscal year; (3) to provide a sufficient flow of continuing funds to finance future-year requests in the capital budget; and (4) to remain within the public's tolerance for higher taxes.

Bill Harper thought through his options. He listed the following alternative strategies on his notepad:

1. Finance all future capital improvements on a "pay-as-you-go" basis.

    This would mean paying for all such improvements in cash during the year they were acquired or constructed. This option would call for tax increases in the years just ahead and also for reduced levels of capital expenditures to minimize the tax increases. But it would eliminate debt service and interest costs, thus keeping total costs for the township down in the long run.

    Because there would be fewer new services and higher taxes in the short

Table 5   Existing debt commitments before capital improvement program

Purpose	Original amount	Term	Current annual debt service
Water project #1	$2,000,000	20 years	$125,000
Water project #2	2,500,000	30 years	100,000
Election-year road construction	1,008,000	10 years	225,000
New municipal building	4,000,000	30 years	180,000

run, this strategy might involve some personal risk for Harper, even though he currently enjoyed solid support from his board.

2. Rely exclusively on short- and long-term debt for all capital expenditures, setting the maturity dates so that each capital expenditure would be financed during its anticipated useful life. (For instance, debt for new utility lines might be repaid over thirty years, while debt for new public works trucks might take five years.)

    Such a strategy would result in heavy debt service costs, but this drawback would be offset by greater fairness: the cost of each expenditure would be paid by the people who actually benefited from its use. Further, while this strategy would involve higher costs in the long run, it would minimize short-term costs. In other words, it would maximize new services now while minimizing short-term tax increases.

3. Fund more capital improvements in cash, reducing the town's reliance on bonded debt.

    Like the first option, this one would require higher taxes now, but the use of some borrowed funds might reduce public opposition to the higher taxes because there would be more services to show for them. This option, a compromise between the first two, sounded attractive to Harper until he remembered that the council already had cut his proposed increase in the cash appropriation for capital expenditures for the next fiscal year by 50 percent.

4. Finance capital improvements with a combination of cash and short-term debt.

    A variant of the third option, this strategy essentially would duplicate the approach used during the current fiscal year: to pay what could be paid from the current fiscal year's cash appropriation, financing the balance with short-term (five-year maximum) borrowing.

    While a good short- and long-term option, this strategy would pose intermediate-range problems. Unless there was substantial growth in the tax base, this technique would leave little or no cash for new public improvements in the third, fourth, and fifth years of its implementation; the short-term debt obligations from earlier years would consume all of the funds customarily budgeted for capital purposes.

While each of these strategies had its advantages, none of them excited Harper. Each also posed major problems. "Which is best?" he mused. "Or is there some other way, some blend of these techniques, that might be developed?"

Discussion questions

1. Did Harper move too quickly to make a decision? Should he have allowed more time to pass, hoping that subsequent events might make the decision easier to make? Explain your answer.

2. Should other actions have been taken to build community support and offset the influence of old-line politicians? Explain your answer.

3. What options, if any, did Harper miss? What advantages and disadvantages of each option did he overlook?

4. How should the goal of providing at least $400,000 in annual capital improvements funding be accomplished?

5. What is the optimal way of funding the capital improvement program? How should the various long- and short-term elements be handled?

6. Evaluate Harper's risks over the tax increase issue. How concerned should he be? Should his personal job security be a factor in his calculation? How much of a tax increase can Harper prudently recommend?

7. What system should be used to incorporate short- or long-term debt into overall funding for the capital improvement program?

List of contributors

James M. Banovetz (Editor) is professor of political science and public administration and director of the Division of Public Administration at Northern Illinois University. Much of the work on this book was accomplished while he held the Albert A. Levin Chair of Urban Studies and Public Service at Cleveland State University. An honorary member of ICMA since 1978 and a past president of Pi Alpha Alpha, the national honorary society in public administration, he has also received the Elmer B. Staats Public Service Career Award from the National Association of Schools of Public Affairs and Administration. The founder of the Cook County Council of Governments and the secretariat of the Illinois City Management Association, he began his career as a member of the staff of the League of Minnesota Municipalities. He holds M.A.P.A. and Ph.D. degrees from the University of Minnesota.

J. Peter Braun (Case 6) is the retired township manager of Randolph Township, New Jersey, and currently director of municipal services for Goodkind & O'Dea, Inc. He previously served as township manager in Middletown and Sparta, New Jersey, and as township administrator in Upper Moreland Township, Pennsylvania. He holds a B.A. degree from Lehigh University and an M.G.A. degree from the Wharton Graduate Division, University of Pennsylvania.

Jon S. Ebeling (Case 3) received his Ph.D. from the Graduate School of Public and International Affairs, University of Pittsburgh, in 1974. He has taught at California State University, Chico, since 1971, where his courses emphasize research methods and statistics and public sector budgeting and finance. He teaches at the graduate and undergraduate levels. His research interests focus on revenue sources for local government. He prefers to research local government problems, and he likes to bring the academic perspective and methods to the analy-

sis of those problems. He served four years in Ethiopia with the U.S. Peace Corps in the 1960s.

Leda McIntyre Hall (Case 1) is an assistant professor of public management in the School of Public and Environmental Affairs at Indiana University South Bend. She is the director of the Institute for Applied Community Research and, in that capacity, acts as advisor and consultant to various local government agencies. Her research is in the areas of urban management and housing policy.

Mary Jane Kuffner Hirt (Case 4) is an assistant professor in the Department of Political Science at Indiana University of Pennsylvania where she teaches graduate and undergraduate courses in state and local political systems, metropolitan problems, leadership and public accountability, research methods, and financial management and supervises the department's internship program. Previously, she served as city manager in the borough of Forest Hills and the township of O'Hara in Pennsylvania. In 1986, she was the first woman to be elected president of the Association for Pennsylvania Municipal Management. She has M.P.A. and Ph.D. degrees from the University of Pittsburgh's Graduate School of Public and International Affairs.

Tom Mills (Case 5) is director of executive education at the Fels Center of Government, University of Pennsylvania. He is a former city official who, during a twenty-two-year career, served as deputy managing director, chief deputy court administrator, and first deputy finance director for the city of Philadelphia. Mills also has been professor of public administration at Fairleigh Dickinson University (Rutherford campus) and is a member of the Philadelphia Board of Education. Mills holds a B.S. degree in economics from the Wharton School, an M.B.A. in industrial management from Drexel University, and an M.A. and Ph.D. in political science from the University of Pennsylvania.

William A. Murphy (Case 3) has served as city manager of Anderson, California (population 8,700), since 1985. He has had experience in several public agencies in California, including manager of the Tahoe Transportation District (1983–85) and administrative assistant for Chico, California (1967–72). Mr. Murphy has B.A. and M.A. degrees from California State University, Chico, and served as administrator and faculty member there from 1972 to 1980. During that period, he was elected to the Chico City Council and served from 1975 to 1979. From 1980 to 1983 he was in practice as a consultant to public and private sectors.

Frederica Shockley (Case 3), chair and professor of economics at California State University, Chico, received her Ph.D. in economics from Georgia State University in 1978. Her primary teaching interests are public finance and managerial economics. In 1994 she implemented one of the first electronic classrooms at CSU in which students use on-line facilities to receive and send assignments. She and her husband, Jon S. Ebeling, have an active consulting practice in northern California where they supply economic forecasts and conduct telephone surveys for local government and private firms. Dr. Shockley specializes in input-output analysis. She has undertaken academic research to determine the impact of developer fees on housing prices.

Bradford J. Townsend (Case 2) is city manager in Wood Dale, Illinois, and has over fifteen years of municipal management experience. He has been a strategic planning consultant, budget director, public works director, and city manager. He has prepared sixteen balanced operating budgets and capital improvement budgets ranging from $10 million to $30 million annually. He has conducted cost-benefit analyses for economic development projects and coordinated the financing of long-term debt. Mr. Townsend earned an M.P.A. with honors from Northern Illinois University and is an honors graduate of Western Illinois University. He is the author of numerous published reports and a member of several professional associations, including ICMA.

Municipal Management Series

**Managing Local
Government Finance:
Cases in
Decision Making**

Text type
Times Roman, Helvetica

Composition
EPS Group Inc.
Easton, Maryland

Printing and binding
Kirby Lithographic Company, Inc.
Washington, D.C.

Design
Herbert Slobin